· THE BOOK OF ·
GARNISHING

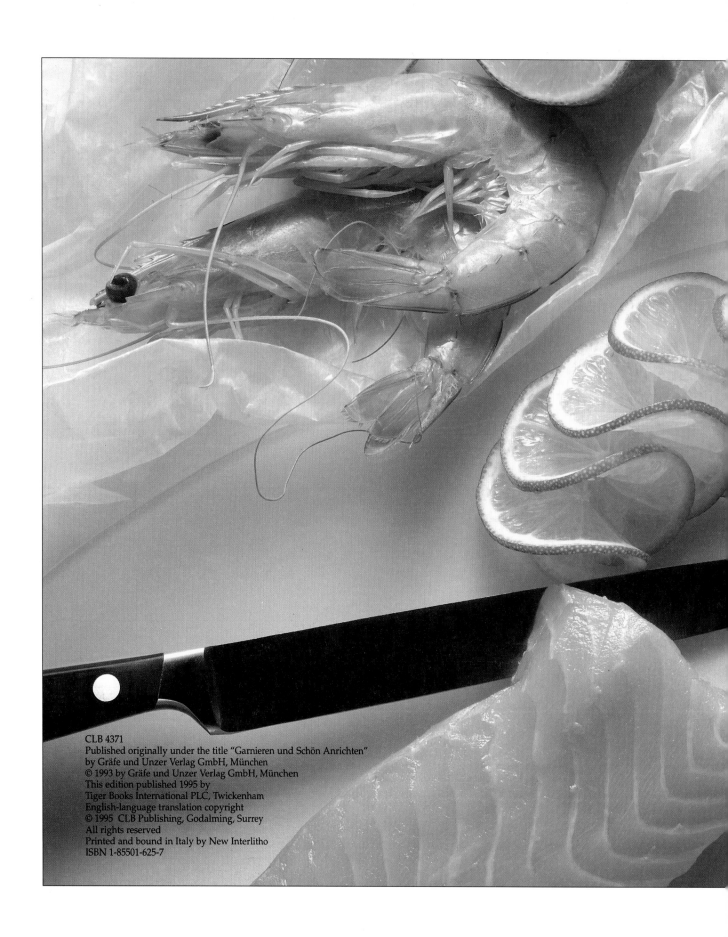

CLB 4371
Published originally under the title "Garnieren und Schön Anrichten"
by Gräfe und Unzer Verlag GmbH, München
© 1993 by Gräfe und Unzer Verlag GmbH, München
This edition published 1995 by
Tiger Books International PLC, Twickenham
English-language translation copyright
© 1995 CLB Publishing, Godalming, Surrey
All rights reserved
Printed and bound in Italy by New Interlitho
ISBN 1-85501-625-7

· THE BOOK OF ·
GARNISHING

CHRISTA SCHMEDES

TIGER BOOKS INTERNATIONAL
LONDON

Contents

Introduction

It's a well-known fact that a nicely garnished meal tastes twice as good. If you are entertaining guests, the presentation of a successful meal should be a pleasant surprise – but don't worry, the days of fussy food decoration are long gone. This book will introduce you to ideas and techniques which will help you to produce effective, attractive dishes, by using simple ingredients, and without using a lot of equipment or taking up much time. You will find a recipe to suit every occasion, with each one as easy to make as the next. This will make clear to you which type of garnish suits which recipe, and of course you are free to try out any combination you like. There are also lots of tips and tricks relating to decorating and garnishing to help you avoid any culinary mishaps. It really isn't difficult to produce little culinary delights. You don't have to be artistic or good at handicrafts, you don't need a lot of kitchen equipment, and you will be amazed how easy it is to create miniature masterpieces. Often all that is needed to produce a pleasing effect is a clever combination of colours and shapes in the ingredients. Let yourself be inspired by the many ideas, suggestions and recipes in this book, then sit back and wait for the praise from your guests!

The chief cookery assistants

Slicing, peeling and chopping

These utensils are essential for skilled work.

• Vegetable knife
You need this type of knife for cutting vegetables to shape. It has a slightly curved blade.

• Patterned knife
This knife has a serrated blade with deep indentations and is used to cut patterns in fruit, vegetables and butter.

• Filleting knife
The filleting knife has a flexible blade which helps to cut meat or fish into fine strips or slices without difficulty.

• Cook's knife
A cook's knife is essential for slicing and chopping meat and vegetables.

• Serrated knife
The long blade is particularly useful for slicing tomatoes and other soft fruit and vegetables.

• Boning knife
With a boning knife you can remove the skin expertly from fish or take bones out of meat.

• Chopping blade
A double-bladed chopper is the simple and swift answer to finely chopped herbs and onions.

• Vegetable peeler
Use to peel potatoes, cucumbers, other vegetables and fruit, with little wastage.

Vegetable knife

Patterned knife

Filleting knife

Cook's knife

Serrated knife

Boning knife

- Butter curler
Used to scrape decorative rolls of butter from the block.

- Cannel knife
Used to peel single wide strips from the skins of oranges, lemons and cucumbers or to cut different types of vegetables into julienne strips.

- Apple corer
Used to remove the cores from apples and similar fruit.

- Apple slicer
Slices apples into equal portions and removes core at the same time.

- Lemon zester
This cuts several fine strips at once from lemon, orange or lime peel. The zest of citrus fruits can be used to decorate various dishes (see page 77, on right).

- Parisian scoop (large), Solferino scoop (small)

- Mandolin cutter
This has various slicing attachments and is used to prepare vegetables such as cucumber, white cabbage, courgettes and also root vegetables for use in salads.

- Linoleum knife
A linoleum knife can be used to decorate hard rinds, such as melon rind, for example.

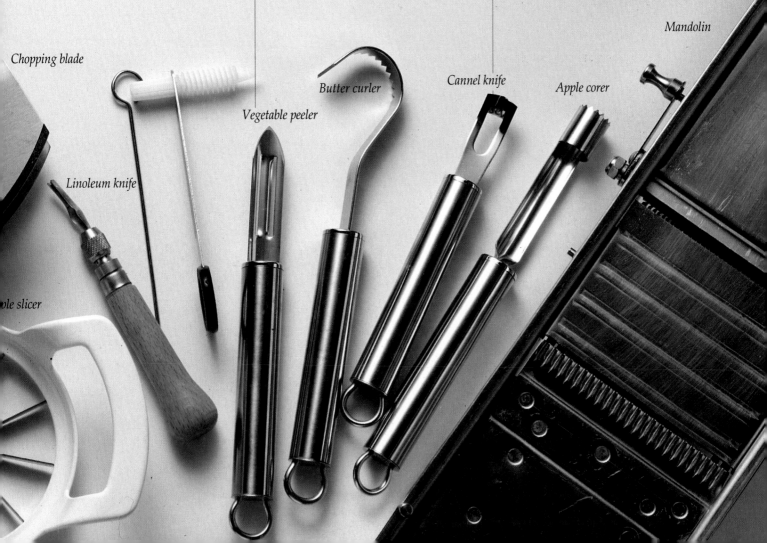

Mandolin

Chopping blade

Butter curler

Cannel knife

Apple corer

Vegetable peeler

Linoleum knife

ole slicer

Shaping, piping and cutting out

This equipment will help you to prepare food attractively.

- Piping bag
Cream and custard cream can be piped in decorative patterns using different-sized round or serrated nozzles.

- Cornet mould for puff pastry
Cornet moulds can be bought from good kitchenware shops. They can be used to roll out puff pastry evenly.

- Round pastry cutters
Used to cut precise circles in different sizes out of jellies, aspic, bread and vegetables.

- Decorative pastry cutters
Used to cut out puff pastry, short-crust pastry and vegetable shapes.

- Palette knives.
Different sizes of palette knives are useful for smoothing glazes and custard fillings. They are also suitable for removing cakes or pastries from a baking sheet.

- Hand mixer

From top to bottom:
Piping bag and different nozzles
Pastry cutters
Cornet moulds
Palette knives
Hand mixer
Special dual sieve

Moulds of all shapes and sizes

You can make very pretty cakes, puddings and moulded rice just by using different types of moulds. Specialist kitchenware shops stock a wide selection. An extensive range of ready-made edible moulds which can be used for fillings is also available.

Large moulds

• Various jelly moulds
You can use the moulds to "style" not only sweet dishes such as blancmanges, mousses and semolina, but also boiled rice.

• Heart-shaped moulds
Suitable for cakes or set custards. Available in stainless steel, earthenware and china.

• Clover leaf moulds
The clover leaf shape is excellent for blancmanges, mousses and cakes. This type of mould is also available in various materials.

• Balmoral tin
This square tin has curved, ridged sides with a straight channel along the base. It is suitable for substantial dishes which are turned out, such as rice, aspic and patés.

• Gugelhupf tin
A classic shape for cakes and desserts.

Individual moulds

• Timbale moulds
Stainless steel timbale moulds are used for rice, jellies and custards.

• Praline moulds
Used to prepare chocolates or candied fruits. Prepared pralines can be displayed in paper or aluminium sweet cases, which are available in different colours.

• Savarin moulds
Metal savarin moulds are suitable for fruit jellies, small rice rings and custards.

• Earthenware moulds and dishes

Earthenware dishes are excellent for preparation of mousses and puddings, and for browning small dishes and hors d'oeuvres.

• Skewers
To prepare fruit, vegetables and chunks of meat attractively, you can choose from wooden skewers (toothpick, kebab skewer), plastic cocktail sticks or metal skewers.

Edible moulds

• Tartlets
You can buy sweet or savoury tartlets, depending on the type of filling you want to use. They can be used in many ways and taste just as good filled with prawns as with fruit.

• Boats
Short-crust pastry boats (sweet or savoury) are suitable for hors d'oeuvres or desserts.

• Mini-croustades, taco shells, mini- and full-sized vol-au-vents are just a few of the ready-made products which are currently available in the shops. They are all very good when complemented by tasty fillings.

Shrimp boats

Makes 8 boats:
100 g/4 oz fresh shrimps
1 tbsp brandy
salt
white pepper
1 head dandelion leaves
(or frisée or radicchio)
8 short-crust pastry boats (ready
made)

Approx. 460 kJ/110 kcal per boat

Preparation time: approx. 15 minutes
(+ ½ hour marinating time)

1. Marinate the shrimps in the
brandy, salt and pepper for about ½
hour.

2. Meanwhile wash, prepare and
shred the dandelion leaves.

3. Fill the short-crust boats with
dandelion leaves and shrimps.

Pictured from left to right:
Gugelhupf tin
Heart-shaped moulds
Large and small savarin moulds
Balmoral tin
Timbale moulds
Praline moulds
Skewers
Earthenware moulds

Vegetable vol-au-vents

Makes 12 vol-au-vents:
2 carrots
1 courgette
1 leek
1 tbsp oil
salt
pepper
1 tbsp herb vinegar
½ bunch parsley
1 tbsp crème fraiche
12 mini vol-au-vents (ready made)

Approx. 520 kJ/120 kcal per vol-au-vent

Preparation time: approx. 30 minutes

1. Peel the carrots and slice finely
lengthways using a mandolin cutter,
then cut into thin strips. Wash the
courgette, slice thinly lengthways
using mandolin and then cut into thin
strips. Cut the leek in half lengthways,
wash thoroughly and cut into fine
strips. Only use the white of the leek.

2. Heat the oil in a frying pan and
sweat the vegetables briefly in the oil.
Add salt, pepper and vinegar and
leave to cool.

3. Wash, dry and finely chop the
parsley. Mix with crème fraiche. Fill
the vol-au-vents with the vegetables
and top each with a blob of crème
fraiche.

From the herb garden

Flowers and leaves

Many plants and herbs possess very pretty flowers or leaves which can be used to decorate a dish without going to a lot of trouble. An added advantage is that they taste good, are full of vitamins, and are good for you. You don't need a garden in order to have fresh herbs to hand always. The various herbs will also grow in little flower boxes or clay pots in a well-lit spot in your home.

- **Nasturtium flowers**
In season: June to September
Nasturtium flowers are an unusual decoration for salads and hors d'oeuvres. The leaves have a spicy taste; the flowers are suitable for decoration and can be eaten too.

- **Courgette flowers**
In season: June to September
Courgette flowers are superb when filled with veal forcemeat, salmon mousse or vegetable fillings. They can also be used for hors d'oeuvres and salads, or as an accompaniment to fish dishes. The flowers need to be steamed for only a short time.

- **Sage**
In season: June to November
Sage leaves have a strong scent and should be used sparingly. The edible flowers are very decorative. Sage goes well with veal, fish dishes, tomatoes, salads and herb sauces.

- **Thyme**
In season: May to November
Thyme flowers are edible and make wonderful decorations. Thyme tastes good with sheep's and goat's cheese, lamb, game and potatoes, and in marinades.

- **Lemon balm**
In season: April to November
Lemon balm goes well with sweets and other dishes which are flavoured with lemon. The leaves are suitable as a garnish for many sweet dishes.

- **Mint**
In season: May to October
Mint goes exceptionally well with sweet dishes, but should be used sparingly. The leaves can be used as a garnish for various recipes.

- **Borage**
In season: May to October
Edible blue borage flowers can be used for special decorations. The leaves should always be used fresh and chopped finely. This typical salad seasoning harmonises well with cucumber, leafy salads, soups and herb sauces.

Nasturtium flowers

Courgette

Sage

Tarragon

Lemon balm

Thyme

Mint

- Dill
In season: May to September
Dill has a delicate aromatic perfume and goes well with shellfish, cucumber, potatoes, meat and fish dishes. The flower clusters can be used for decoration.

- Chives
In season: April to November
Chives are an ideal addition to sandwiches, consommés, potatoes, onion dishes and salads. They are finely chopped and sprinkled over the dishes, and should only be used raw. Chives have very decorative pale purple flowers. Chive stalks are excellent for tying up bundles of vegetables.

- Chinese chives
In season: can be bought all year round from Chinese food shops
The stem smells slightly of garlic. The attractive star-shaped white flowers are edible. Chinese chives can be used in salads, soups and various dishes where a hint of garlic is required. They should always be used raw.

- Sorrel
In season: March to December
The tender green sorrel leaves taste slightly acidic. Sorrel is used in soups, sauces, vegetable and fish dishes. The arrow-shaped leaves are suitable as a garnish for fish dishes or salads.

- Daisies and wild violets
Daisies and wild violets are welcome edible decorations. They are found in fields and gardens. You should take care, however, not to use flowers which are growing next to a busy road or in cultivated fields (because of lead contamination and fertilisers).

- Other leaves
Banana leaves (available from Asian shops), rose leaves and vine leaves are very good for decorative purposes.

Chinese chives

Chives

Sorrel

Rose

Daisies

Banana leaves

Dill

Violets

Every skilled cook has a trick up his or her sleeve to help make work in the kitchen that bit easier. Here are a few tips which should prevent culinary disasters or be useful in other ways.

Separating fat from stock
Line a sieve with a cloth and place ice cubes in the bottom. Sieve the cooled stock until globules of fat are no longer visible.

Blanching vegetables
To blanch vegetables, bring plenty of water to the boil with a dash of vinegar. Plunge the prepared vegetables into the boiling water for a few minutes. Then plunge into ice-cold water and drain on kitchen paper. In this way the vegetables will retain their colour.

Artichokes
Always rub cut surfaces of artichokes with lemon juice so they don't discolour.

Avocados
Puréed avocado flesh will not discolour if you leave the stone in the purée until just before serving.

Cleaning mushrooms
Never put mushrooms in water; they soak up too much liquid. If necessary, clean mushrooms under running water.

Boiling noodles and pasta
Boiled noodles won't stick if you add a drop of oil to them.

Storing oil
Olive oil should not be stored in the refrigerator. The oil becomes viscous and the colour changes.

Fruit and gelatine
Dishes which use gelatine won't set if you use raw kiwi fruit, pineapple or mango. Simmer the fresh fruit for about 3 minutes first.

Turning out gelatine dishes
Dishes containing gelatine can be loosened from the mould and turned out more easily if the underside of the mould is dipped briefly in hot water.

Fruit and colour
Peaches, apricots and nectarines will retain their colour if poached briefly in boiling water with lemon juice added to it.

Fruit and milk products
Fresh pineapple, kiwi fruit and mangoes taste bitter if used raw in dishes which include milk products. The fruit contains a enzyme that breaks down protein; it is only neutralised if the fruit is poached first.

Turning out blancmange and mousses
Before filling the mould with mousse, rinse it out with cold water. When you want to turn the mousse out, it will come away easily from the mould.

Melting chocolate over hot water.
You will always melt chocolate successfully if you add a little coconut oil. But beware – if chocolate comes into contact with water when melted, it turns grey and lumpy.

Quick – but still decorative

Sometimes you just don't have enough time to spend ages decorating a meal. If this is the case, then these quick and easy decorations, which are suitable for almost any recipe and which you can always prepare in advance, will surely help.

Tea eggs
Bring 1 litre/1¾ pints water to the boil with 2 tbsps tea leaves and 2 tbsps soy sauce. Hard-boil the eggs. Press down on the eggs shells so that they crack all over but don't break off. Place the eggs in the tea infusion and simmer for about 45 minutes. Leave to cool in the liquid. Carefully shell the eggs. The eggs are an ideal decoration for salads.

Palm hearts
Remove palm hearts from tin, drain, and cut into slices.

Shallots Van Dyke
Peel the shallots, cut in half lengthways and cut a V-shape in the pointed top of the shallot, to make two points.

Filled tomatoes
Wash and halve a small tomato, then remove seeds and flesh. Fill with pumpkin seeds.

Orange peel shapes
Wash an orange and peel thinly. Cut out shapes as desired from orange peel.

Lemon flowers
Wash a lemon and, using a sharp knife, cut around the lemon, working through to the middle, in a zig-zag shape (Van Dyke pattern). Push the lemon halves together and twist each half in the opposite direction so the two halves are separated.

Lemon roses
Wash a lemon and peel thinly. Twist the lemon peel to form a flower shape.

Lemon spirals
Wash a lemon and cut into slices. Make a cut from the edge of each slice into the centre. Bend the lemon slice on either side of the cut to form a twist. Link several twists together to form a spiral.

Lime zest
Wash a lime and peel off thin strips of rind using a zester.

Additional decorations
There really aren't any other decorations which are faster to make than these. However, the following can be scattered over the prepared dish:

- sunflower seeds for salads
- pumpkin seeds for soups and salads
- star anise for sweet dishes.

Cheese mushrooms

Makes about 20 mushrooms:
2 slices mature Gouda
(approx. ½ cm / ¼ inch thick)
1 cucumber
paprika
lettuce and other salad leaves to taste

Approx. 280 kJ / 67 kcal per piece

Preparation time: approx. 10 minutes

1. Cut out mushroom shapes from the cheese using a shaped cutter.

2. Wash the cucumber and cut away strips from the peel using a lemon zester. Then cut the cucumber into slices approx. 1 cm / ½ inch thick.

3. Lay the cheese mushrooms on top of the cucumber slices and dust with paprika. Arrange on a plate with lettuce and other salad leaves as desired.

Variation: cheese rings

Cut out approx. 16 circles from 300 g / 11 oz holey cheese (from 2 slices approx. 1 cm / ½ inch thick), using a fluted cutter, 4 cm / 1¾ inches in diameter. Cut a hole in the middle of each circle of cheese using a smaller cutter, approx. 1 cm / ½ inch in diameter. Place a green or black grape in the middle of each ring. Make a small cut in the top of other grapes and slot a small circle of cheese into each cut.

Puff pastry

Choux pastry

Short-crust pastry

Delicious-tasting cases for sweet and savoury fillings can be made from pastry.

Choux pastry

Serves 4:
250 ml/8 fl. oz water
pinch salt
60 g/2 oz butter
150 g/6 oz flour
4 eggs

Approx. 1500 kJ/360 kcal per person

Preparation time: approx. 20 minutes
(+ 35-40 minutes cooking time)

1. Bring the water to the boil in a pan with the salt and butter. Add all the flour to the boiling liquid at once, beating constantly with a wooden spoon until a ball of dough forms and a white film is deposited on the edge of the pan.

2. Stir in the eggs one by one. A ball of dough should form every time. The dough will shine and form long strands when the wooden spoon is removed from the mixture. Preheat the oven to 200° C/400°F/Gas mark 6.

3. Line a baking sheet with baking parchment and, using teaspoons, break off portions of the dough and place them on the baking sheet; or fill a piping bag with the pastry and, using different nozzles, pipe ribbons or rosettes onto the baking sheet. Bake in the centre of the oven for 35-40 minutes. Don't open the oven door during the first 20 minutes of cooking time, or the pastry will sink.

4. Leave the pastry to cool, then, using a pointed knife, cut off a lid from each pastry case. Cream, custard cream, savoury cheese filling, ragout and many other fillings can be used.

Short-crust pastry

Serves 4:
200 g/7 oz butter
100 g/4 oz caster sugar
2 egg yolks
300 g/11 oz flour
For the work surface:
flour

Basic recipe for sweet fillings

Approx. 3300 kJ/790 kcal per person

Preparation time: approx. 20 minutes
(+ 10-15 minutes cooking time)

1. Cream together butter and sugar until light and fluffy. Add the egg yolks and continue beating until the mixture is creamy. Add the flour, and knead everything together quickly to form short-crust pastry. Wrap in cling film and refrigerate for a few minutes.

2. Preheat the oven to 175°C/350°F/Gas mark 4. Roll out the pastry on a lightly floured work surface. Cut out the pastry using a tartlet tin or another shape. Prick all over with a fork.

3. Use the pastry to line a greased tin, or bake on a baking sheet in the centre of the oven for 10-15 minutes.

4. Leave to cool. Fill with fruit, cream, fruit-flavoured curd cheese or other fillings.

Variation: short-crust pastry for savoury fillings
Make the dough from 250 g/9 oz flour, 150 g/6 oz butter, 1 egg and a pinch of salt.

Puff pastry

You won't panic at an unexpected visit if you have puff pastry in your freezer, which you can quickly use to make all kinds of delicacies. Puff pastry is tasty with either sweet or savoury fillings, or simply sprinkled with caraway and cheese.

1. Allow the puff pastry to thaw out, then roll out on a floured work surface to approximately double the size. Cut out an even number of stars, hearts, triangles or circles.

2. Cut out the middle from half of the shapes of each type. Brush these shapes with egg white and place, egg-white side down, on top of one of the same whole shape, to form a raised border. Brush with egg yolk.

3. Place on a baking sheet lined with baking parchment and bake in the centre of a preheated oven at 220°C/425°F/Gas mark 7 for about 20 minutes. Sprinkle the cut-out shapes with caraway, sesame seeds or grated cheese and bake. When baked, fill shapes as liked.

Variation: puff pets
Roll out a block of pastry to a rectangle approx. 4 mm/½ inch thick. Cut into strips 1 cm wide and 30 cm long/⅜ inch x 12 inches. Wrap the strips around a cornet mould. Brush the overlapping edges of the strips with water so that they stick together. If you haven't got a cornet mould, cut the sheet of pastry into squares and roll up, working diagonally from one corner towards the opposite corner. Place the cornets on a baking sheet lined with baking parchment and refrigerate for 1 hour. Brush with egg yolk. Bake at 220° C/425°F/Gas mark 7 for about 25 minutes. The cornets can be filled with vegetables and cream cheese, or with jam or whipped cream.

Aspic is easily made from gelatine and liquid, and can be cut into various shapes such as dice or circles. It is a flexible garnish, and not just used for a platter of cold meats. Fruit, salami and cold sausage can all be coated in aspic.

Sherry aspic

Ingredients for a mould of about 500 ml/16 fl. oz capacity:
10 leaves gelatine
500 ml/16 fl. oz clear meat stock
20 ml/2 tbsps sherry

Basic recipe

1. Soften the gelatine in cold water.

2. Heat the meat stock and sherry together, remove the gelatine from the water, stir into the stock and dissolve. Pour the liquid into a mould or a deep plate and refrigerate.

3. When the aspic has set, cut out shapes using cutters or cut into different-sized dice.

Variation: aspic sheet
If you want to make a sheet of aspic, only use 8 leaves of gelatine. If you want to coat fruit in a layer of aspic, you should use water or fruit juice instead of meat stock.

Herb aspic

Ingredients for a mould of about 500 ml/16 fl. oz capacity:
10 leaves gelatine
250 ml/8 fl. oz fish stock
250 ml/8 fl. oz white wine
To garnish:
parsley leaves, dill fronds

1. Soften the gelatine in cold water.

2. Mix together the fish stock and white wine and heat. Remove the gelatine from the water, stir into the liquid and dissolve.

3. Pour the liquid into ice cube

moulds or other moulds as wished.

Place the leaves and dill fronds in the aspic just before it sets.

Fruit aspic

Ingredients for a mould of about 500 ml/16 fl. oz capacity:
8 leaves gelatine
500 ml/16 fl. oz fruit juice

1. Soften the gelatine in cold water.

2. Heat the fruit juice. Remove the gelatine from the water, add to the fruit juice and allow to dissolve. Pour the liquid into individual praline moulds or 1 large mould.

3. When the aspic has set, cut out shapes as wished.

Tip
You can also prepare the fruit jellies by using packet jellies (available in various shades, including red, yellow and green).

Mini-brawns with quails' eggs

Makes 12 brawns:
1 quantity sherry aspic (page 22)
6 quails' eggs
1 bunch tarragon
12 slices white bread
30 g/1 oz lamb's lettuce (or corn salad)
radishes if wished
12 egg cups

Approx. 330 kJ/79 kcal per brawn

Preparation time: approx. 30 minutes
(+ chilling time)

1. Prepare the sherry aspic according to the basic recipe.

2. Cook the quails' eggs in boiling water for about 8 minutes until hard. Plunge into cold water, remove shells and cut in half.

3. Strip the tarragon leaves from the stalks and plunge briefly into hot water. Rinse out the egg cups with cold water and pour in a little liquid aspic. Leave in the refrigerator to set.

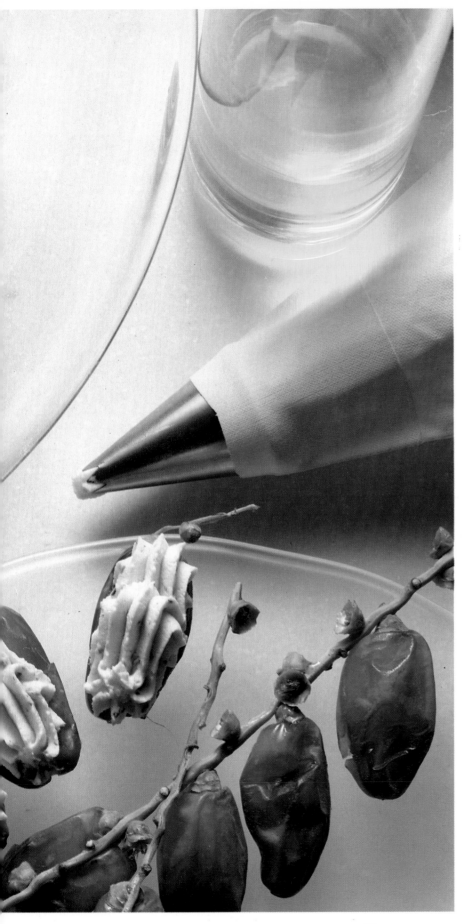

Hors d'oeuvres and salads

Every celebratory meal starts with an hors d'oeuvre. They provide an introduction to the main menu, whether they consist of delicious nibbles, a colourful salad or a surprise morsel wrapped in pastry or leaves. The following chapter contains ideas and suggestions. Give your guests a treat right from the start and surprise them with a prelude to the main event which is as easy on the eye as it is delicious.

A feast for the eyes – butter and cream cheese

Butter and cream cheese belong on every buffet table next to the bread basket.

Butter

Serves 4:
200 g/7 oz unsalted butter
salt
freshly ground white pepper

Mix the butter, which should be slightly soft, with the salt and pepper. Then flavour as wished and use to fill pretty china dishes or mussel shells.

Variations
Use the same quantity as in the basic recipe and add the ingredients given below.

• Herb butter
2 tbsps chopped herbs
1 tsp lemon juice

• Shrimp butter
2 tbsps minced shrimps
1 tsp cognac
shrimps for decoration

• Lemon butter
1 tbsp lemon juice
rind of ½ lemon
lemon zest for decoration

• Olive butter
1 tbsp finely chopped black olives
olives and chives for decoration

• Anchovy butter
1 tbsp minced anchovies
rolled anchovies for decoration

• Garlic butter
3 crushed garlic cloves

Butter rolls
Scrape strips from a block of chilled butter using a butter curler.

Coloured butter balls
Shape the butter into little balls. Roll ⅓ of balls in chopped cress, ⅓ in sesame seeds and the rest in paprika.

Butter moulds
Soak little wooden butter moulds for about ½ hour. Fill with butter which is at room temperature, pressing the butter well down into the mould. Refrigerate, then turn the butter out of the moulds and arrange.

Butter roses
Roll out the chilled butter between 2 sheets of greaseproof paper until approx. 3 mm/⅛ inch thick. Cut out 8 circles, 4 cm/1½ inches in diameter. To make the heart of the flower, make a small ball out of butter. Position the bottom of each circle against the base of the ball to form the petals, pressing down lightly to make petals stick. When all petals are in position, immerse the finished rose in iced water until just before serving.

Cream cheese

Cream cheese looks pretty served on nasturtium leaves or accompanied by celery sticks and slices of orange and cucumber. For a children's party you could make a cream cheese mouse with a tail made out of chives, and a hedgehog with spines made out of flaked almonds.

Serves 4:
200 g/7 oz cream cheese
50 g/2 oz cream
salt

Mix together the cream cheese and cream, and season with salt. Then display attractively or flavour as follows.

Variations
Use the same quantity as in the basic recipe and add the appropriate ingredients.

• Paprika cream cheese
1 finely chopped onion
1 tsp ground paprika

• Cream cheese with chives
1 bunch chives, finely chopped
freshly ground white pepper

• Nutty cream cheese
1 tbsp ground cashew nuts
2 tbsps chopped pistachio nuts
1 tbsp lemon juice
curry powder

• Cream cheese with horseradish
2 tbsps freshly grated horseradish
1 tbsp orange juice
1 tsp grated zest of an orange

• Cream cheese with mustard
1 tsp hot mustard
1 tsp grain mustard
1 bunch chopped chives

• Cream cheese with cucumber
1 coarsely grated cucumber
1 tsp white wine vinegar
fresh mint leaves

Clockwise, from top:
butter rose, cream cheese and horseradish balls, cream cheese with chives, paprika cream cheese, olive butter, garlic butter, shrimp butter, anchovy butter, herb butter

You know what it's like – friends have let you know at the last minute that they intend to drop by. You would like to offer them something tasty to go with drinks, but you haven't got time to spend ages cooking. The problem is solved with these nibbles, which are easily made without much preparation, and of course they look great!

Below: tomato and mozzarella kebabs
Top left: artichoke hearts with salmon mousse
Right: dates with gorgonzola cream

Tomato and mozzarella kebabs

Makes 4 kebabs:
8 cherry tomatoes or 2-3 tomatoes
12 basil leaves
8 mini-mozzarella balls
1 tbsp olive oil
freshly ground black pepper
4 metal or wooden skewers

Approx. 620 kJ/150 kcal per kebab

Preparation time: approx 10 minutes

1. Wash the tomatoes and basil leaves and pat dry. If using cherry tomatoes leave them whole, slice other tomatoes into quarters.

2. Alternately thread 2 cherry tomatoes or 2-3 tomato quarters, 2 mozzarella balls and 3 basil leaves onto each skewer. Drizzle olive oil over kebabs and season with pepper.

Artichoke hearts with salmon mousse

Ingredients for 8 hearts:
8 small (tinned) artichoke hearts
100 g/4 oz smoked salmon (approx. 5 slices)
1 tbsp brandy
100 g/4 oz cream
1 bunch dill or 1 box cress
lemon slices if wished

Approx. 310 kJ/74 kcal per heart

Preparation time: approx. 20 minutes

1. Reserve 1 slice of salmon for garnish, then purée remaining salmon together with brandy. Whip the cream until stiff and fold into the salmon purée.

2. Drain the artichoke hearts. Fill a piping bag with the salmon purée and pipe onto the artichoke hearts.

3. Cut the reserved slice of salmon into dice or thin strips. Wash the dill or cress, pat dry and remove leaves from stalks. Garnish the artichoke hearts with dill or cress, lemon slices and strips of salmon.

Tip
You can also use the salmon mousse to fill mini-croustades.

Dates with gorgonzola cream

Ingredients for 12 dates:
12 fresh dates
100 g/4 oz gorgonzola
50 g/2 oz cream
6 stuffed green olives
watercress

Approx. 380 kJ/90 kcal per date

Preparation time: approx. 20 minutes

1. Remove the stones from the dates. Mix together the cream and gorgonzola to form a smooth paste.

2. Fill a piping bag with the cheese mixture and pipe into the dates. Halve the olives. Place half an olive and some watercress on top of the cheese. Secure with a cocktail stick if necessary.

Pumpernickel rounds with nut cream

Makes 8 rounds:
16 pumpernickel rounds or
2 slices dark, wholemeal-type bread
100 g/4 oz mascarpone
50 g/2 oz quark or curd cheese
50 g/2 oz pistachio nuts
1 tsp grated zest from an orange
salt
chives if wished

Approx. 350 kJ/83 kcal per round
Preparation time: approx. 15 minutes

1. Cut out circles 2 cm/1 inch in diameter from half of the pumpernickel rounds, or if using slices of bread cut out 16 rounds, each 4 cm/1½ inches in diameter, then proceed as above.

2. Mix together the curd cheese and mascarpone. Finely chop the pistachio nuts, reserving some for garnish. Mix together the mascarpone cream, chopped pistachio nuts and orange rind. Season with salt.

3. Take a piping bag with a round nozzle and fill with about ⅔ of the cheese mixture. Pipe cheese onto the

Left: pumpernickel rounds with nut cream; right: trout cream

large pumpernickel or bread rounds. Place a smaller round on top of each blob of cheese, then pipe the remaining cheese mixture onto the small rounds and decorate with reserved pistachios and pieces of orange rind and chives, as liked.

Trout cream

Serves 4:
2 smoked trout fillets (approx. 150 g/ approx. 6 oz)
1 tbsp lemon juice
4 leaves gelatine
250 g/9 oz cream
20 ml/2 tbsp sherry
salt
lemon pepper
1 bunch dill
1 tbsp trout roe
cucumber if wished
cling film

Approx. 1200 kJ/290 kcal per person

Preparation time: approx. 30 minutes
(+ 2 hours chilling time)

1. Tear the fillets into small pieces, mix with the lemon juice and blend to a purée in a food processor. Prepare the gelatine according to the instructions on the packet.

2. Whip the cream until stiff, add the sherry and the drained gelatine. Mix cream thoroughly with the fish mousse, season with salt and pepper.

3. Line a square dish with straight sides with greaseproof paper. Fill the dish with trout mousse. Cover and leave to set for about 2 hours in the refrigerator.

4. Meanwhile wash the dill and shake dry, chop up small if required. Turn the mousse out onto a plate, remove the paper and cut into diamonds. Garnish with dill and trout roe and serve on slices of cucumber if wished.

Spring salad

Colourful salads make a refreshing side dish or a light meal on hot days. They are healthy and full of vitamins, while the attractive shapes and colours are a pleasure to eat.

Serves 4:
200 g/7 oz mixed salad leaves (for example, lamb's lettuce/corn salad, radicchio, watercress, garden cress, dandelion leaves); 2 bunches mixed herbs (basil, borage, parsley, chives, lemon balm)
1 tsp medium hot mustard
1 tsp lemon juice
2 tbsps white wine vinegar
salt
freshly ground black pepper
3 tbsps olive oil
nasturtium flowers

Approx. 380 kJ/90 kcal per person

Preparation time: approx. 25 minutes

1. Prepare the salad, wash and pat dry. Tear into bite-sized pieces.

2. Wash the herbs and pat dry. Remove leaves from stalks. Finely chop the chives and borage.

3. Mix the salad and herbs together.

4. Mix the mustard, lemon juice and vinegar to a smooth paste. Season with salt and pepper. Add the oil and mix in a blender or food processor.

5. Arrange the salad on plates or place in a large glass bowl. Pour the dressing over the salad, toss to distribute dressing evenly and garnish with nasturtium flowers.

Tip
Garnish the salad with borage flowers. Use seasonal salads and herbs according to taste.

Mixed salad

Serves 4:
300 g/ 11 oz mixed salad leaves (e.g. romana, frisée, lollo rosso, oak leaf)
1 small leek
2 sticks celery
4 apricots
1 tbsp lemon juice
1½ tbsps honey
(acacia flower honey is best)
50 g/2 oz walnuts
2 tbsps white wine vinegar
2 tbsps sunflower oil
2 tbsps walnut oil
salt
freshly ground white pepper

Approx. 900 kJ/210 kcal per person

Preparation time: approx. 25 minutes

1. Prepare and wash the salad, shake dry and tear into bite-sized pieces. Cut the leek in half, remove the coarse green top. Wash thoroughly and leave to drain. Slice the leek into thin strips and blanch. Wash the celery and cut into thin slices.

2. Wash the apricots, remove the stones, pat dry and slice into sections. Gently heat the lemon juice with 1 tsp honey and marinate the apricots in the honey. Roast the walnuts in a frying pan, without fat, and reserve.

3. To make the dressing, mix the remaining honey with the vinegar. Gradually add the oil, stirring all the time. Season with salt and pepper. Toss the salad in the dressing.

4. Arrange the salad on a plate, scatter strips of leek and slices of celery over salad leaves. Arrange the apricots and walnuts attractively on top of the salad.

Tip
Instead of apricots you could use white peaches or nectarines.
Flat lettuce, iceberg lettuce or endive are also suitable for the salad mix, when in season.

With a little sleight of hand you can conjure original decorations from raw tomatoes, radishes, button mushrooms, mooli and cucumber.

Tomato roses

1. Wash a firm tomato and pat dry. Using a small, sharp knife and starting at the stalk, peel away the skin in a long strip.

2. Wrap the skin around a finger, pull upwards and in this way shape into a rose.

Tomato flowers

1. Wash a cherry tomato and pat dry. Using a sharp, pointed knife, slice down through the skin (not all the way through the tomato) from the stalk to the base in 6 segments.

2. Carefully loosen the skin petals one by one from the tomato and peel down until nearly at the base of the tomato. If wished put a few herbs in the centre of the "flower".

Radish roses

Wash and prepare the radishes. Make short, curving cuts, not too deep, all around the radish. Place the radishes in iced water so the cuts open out to form a rose shape.

Radish flowers

• Slice the radish into sections lengthways, but don't cut through all the way to the bottom. Place in iced water for several hours so the flowers can open out.

• Slice the radish skin into several segments from top to bottom, stopping just before you reach the base. Carefully loosen the skin from the centre of the radish, peeling back to form leaves.

Radish ladybirds

1. Wash the radishes. Remove the stalks and leaves. Carefully divide the roots to make the feelers.

2. Cut 2 leaf-shaped outlines, working from the root to the top. Then cut out the wings.

3. Using a small, pointed knife, decorate the body with dots or stripes.

Variations on mushrooms

• Clean the mushrooms thoroughly with kitchen paper. Remove the stalks. Using a cannel knife, cut 6 stripes from the centre of each mushroom head down to the edge. Sprinkle with lemon juice.

• Using a sharp knife, and working from the centre of the mushroom, make crescent-shaped cuts side by side around the mushroom. Sprinkle with lemon juice so the mushrooms don't discolour.

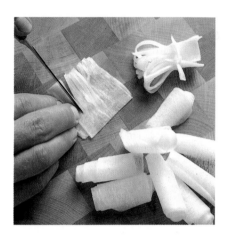

Mooli bows

Wash the mooli and cut long, thin slices lengthways using a mandolin cutter. Season the long slices with salt and shape into rolls, flowers or bows. Or you can fold over the slices of mooli and cut an end into a fringe. Then use a strip of mooli to tie up in a roll.

Mooli rose

1. From an evenly shaped mooli cut off a piece approx. 6 cm/2 inches in length and peel thinly. Working around the piece of mooli, make a single cut from the top to near the bottom. This will form the outer layers of petals.

2. Working towards the centre, cut further petals, staggering them as you cut. Using scissors, trim the petals until they are fairly even. Bend the external petals outwards slightly. Place the rose in water so that it opens up.

Tip

You can also place the rose in beetroot juice to colour it red, or just colour the lower half.

Decorations using cucumber

• Wash the cucumber and cut in half lengthways. Cut the cucumber into wafer-thin slices, but don't slice through completely until each sixth slice. Press down gently with a finger tip to make the cucumber slices fan out.

• Wash and peel the cucumber. Using a Solferino scoop, cut out little balls.

• Wash the cucumber. Using a cannel knife, cut notches in the cucumber and then slice.

• Wash the cucumber and slice in half lengthways. Cut into 6 cm/2-inch-long pieces. Make wafer-thin cuts lengthways in the cucumber chunks, but don't cut all the way through. Fold every second cucumber slice in to the middle.

Peppers of all colours

• Wash the pepper and cut off the stalk. Using a knife, remove the seeds and cut the pepper into slices.

• Wash the pepper, slice in half, and remove core and stalk. You should be left with a flat surface. Cut out diamond shapes, or use cutters to make circles, leaves and flowers.

• Wash and clean several different-coloured peppers. Slice the peppers into thin strips. Using chives, tie 1 red, 1 green and 1 yellow strip of pepper together in the middle to form a bundle.

Carrot bundles

Peel the carrots and slice into finger-long pieces. Then cut into thin slices, and then into thin matchsticks. Blanch briefly, then, using chives, tie up into bundles.

All kinds of sprouts

(bean sprouts, mustard and cress sprouts, alfalfa sprouts)
Rinse the sprouts well and leave to drain. They are particularly decorative if sprinkled over a green salad.
Hors d'oeuvres in "envelopes" are decorative and can also surprise with their hidden fillings.

Pastry parcels

Makes 8 parcels:
8 spring roll wrappers (deep frozen)
2 spring onions
100 g/4 oz bean sprouts
200 g/7 oz minced meat
50 g/2 oz prawns
2 tbsps soy sauce
1 tsp hot chilli sauce
or sambal olek
freshly ground black pepper
For sautéing and deep frying
oil

Approx. 1500 kJ/360 kcal per parcel

Preparation time: about 50 minutes

1. Allow the pastry to thaw, then spread out the sheets of pastry next to each other. Cover with a damp cloth so they don't dry out.

2. Wash and clean the spring onions, then chop finely. Wash and drain the bean sprouts.

3. Heat 1-2 tbsps oil in a frying pan. Fry the minced meat. Add the prawns and vegetables. Season with soy sauce, chilli sauce and pepper. Leave to cool.

4. Put 1 tsp filling in the middle of each sheet of pastry. Shape the pastry into parcels.

5. Heat the oil in a deep fat fryer or deep pan. To prevent the parcels coming apart, secure the parcels with two wooden skewers. Dip in the hot oil and fry for about 3 minutes until done. If wished tie up with strips of spring onion to decorate.

Stuffed vine leaves

Serves 6:
40 vine leaves (tinned)
2 shallots
6 tbsps cold-pressed olive oil
150 g/6 oz wild rice
500 ml/16 fl. oz vegetable stock
1 bunch mixed herbs (dill, parsley, mint)
50 g/2 oz pine kernels
50 g/2 oz raisins
juice and rind of 1 organic lemon
salt

Approx. 1100 kJ/260 kcal per person

Preparation time: about 1¾ hours
(+ 6 hours chilling time)

1. Place the vine leaves briefly in hot water, remove and leave to drain. Peel and finely chop the shallots.

2. Heat 3 tbsp oil, sweat the shallots and rice in the oil until transparent. Add the stock, cover and simmer over a low heat for about 35 minutes.

3. Meanwhile wash the herbs, shake dry and chop finely. Roast the pine kernels in a frying pan without fat, leave to cool and chop coarsely. Wash and drain the raisins.

4. Add the herbs, pine kernels, raisins and lemon rind to the rice, turn off the cooker, leave to combine for about 5 minutes, then season with salt.

5. Fill ½ of the vine leaves with 1 tbsp rice. The smooth side should face outwards. Fold over the vine leaves, then roll up.

6. Line a large pan with the remaining vine leaves. Place the filled vine leaves inside. Mix the remaining oil with the lemon juice and 750 ml/1¼ pints water, pour over the vine leaves, cover and simmer for 50 minutes. The stuffed vine leaves taste best if refrigerated overnight.

Leaves as wrappings and fillings

A whole range of leaves is suitable as a casing for different types of fillings. Just let your tastebuds and your imagination run riot.

- Nori leaves (Japanese seaweed, available from specialist shops)
- Spinach leaves
- Chard leaves
- Savoy cabbage leaves
- Rice paper (available from specialist shops)
- Ready-made pastry sheets in various sizes from specialist Oriental food shops
1. Won-tons (small sheets of pastry, used in soups)
2. Spring roll wrappers
3. Strudel pastry

Different ways of using casings
(Boiled rice is a suitable filling for all the casings.)

- Nori leaves
Stuff the leaves and roll up or shape into cornets.

- Spinach leaves
Shape blanched leaves into little rolls.

- Chard leaves
Stuff blanched leaves with filling. Use small sausages or eggs on their own, or layer with rice, roll up and slice.

- Savoy cabbage leaves
Blanch the leaves, stuff and shape into parcels. Cut green leaves into strips and use to tie up the parcels.

- Rice paper
Soften the rice paper in water until transparent. Then fill and shape into rolls or cornets. Tie up with chives or strips of spring onion.

- Noodle pastry
Can easily be folded up to form an envelope.

- Savoury bonbons
Use noodle pastry or rice paper. When filled, roll up and tie at each end with thin strips of pastry to form a bonbon shape.

Nori leaves

Savoury bonbons

Noodle envelopes

Rice paper

Stuffed spinach leaves

Stuffed chard leaves

Stuffed Savoy cabbage leaves

Sushi

Sushi is a type of Japanese hors d'oeuvre. It can be eaten with an aperitif or as an appetizer between courses. Original Japanese sushi is made with marinated raw fish.

Serves 6:
500 g/1 lb 2 oz rice
(sushi rice is available from specialist Oriental food stores)
2 tbsps rice vinegar (or wine vinegar)
1 tsp sugar
1 avocado
1 lemon
100 g/4 oz smoked salmon
4 nori leaves
20 g/1 oz salmon roe
For garnish:
Chinese chives flowers
banana leaves

Approx. 1800 kJ/430 kcal per person

Preparation time: about 1½ hours
(+ 1 hour chilling time)

1. Bring the rice to the boil in a covered pan with plenty of water, then leave to simmer on a low heat for 25 minutes. Leave to swell a little. Fill a large bowl with the warm rice.

2. Mix together sugar and vinegar, and heat gently in a small pan until the sugar has dissolved. Mix with the rice, cover and leave to cool.

3. Peel the avocado, remove stone and cut flesh into strips. Squeeze the lemon and drizzle lemon juice over avocado slices. Cut the salmon into thin strips.

4. Place 3 nori leaves on a tea towel. Shape the rice into 3 rolls and divide between the nori leaves. Put the salmon on top of 1 rice roll, and avocado on another. The third roll is left plain. Using the tea towel to help you, roll up the nori leaves and refrigerate for 1 hour or unxtil thoroughly chilled.

5. Using a sharp knife, slice the rolls into 3 cm/1 inch long strips.

6. Place the rolls in a lacquered box or on a pretty tray. Decorate the plain rice roll with salmon roe. Cut the remaining nori leaf into decorative shapes and use to garnish the rice rolls. Make further decorations out of chive flowers and banana leaves, and serve with chilled soy sauce.

Tip
The rolls look nice if served on a bed of bean sprouts.
The rice rolls can also be wrapped in spinach or chard leaves.

These filled delicacies are ideal both for cold buffets and other occasions and don't take much effort to prepare.

Stuffed eggs

Serves 2:
4 eggs
80 g/3 oz crème fraiche
salt
curry powder

Approx. 1600 kJ/380 kcal per person

Preparation time: approx. 25 minutes

1. Cook the eggs in boiling water for about 10 minutes until hard. Rinse in cold water, leave to cool, then shell.

2. Slice the eggs in half lengthways and carefully remove the yolk from each egg. Mix the egg yolk with the crème fraiche, salt and curry powder, if necessary using a hand mixer to blend to a smooth paste.

3. Put the egg mixture in a piping bag with a star-shaped nozzle and pipe into the egg whites. Decorate each egg half differently and arrange on a large plate.

• Place a slice of cucumber on top of each egg white and pipe the yolks on top of this.

• Pipe the egg yolk mixture into the egg white, then dot caviar around the edge.

• Pipe the egg yolks onto the egg whites in a rosette shape, then smooth over and place 1 dill frond or a lattice pattern made of chives on top of the egg yolk mixture.

• Place 1 small salad leaf on the egg white, and pipe the egg yolk mixture in a spiral pattern on top.

Stuffed avocados

Serves 4:
2 avocados
1 lime
250 g/9 oz cream
salt
freshly ground white pepper
1 tsp brandy if desired
red peppercorns if desired

Approx. 1800 kJ/430 kcal per person

Preparation time: approx. 20 minutes

1. Halve the avocados, remove the stones, and carefully scrape flesh out of the skins.

2. Wash the lime, remove the zest and squeeze. Sprinkle lime juice over the avocado, then purée.

3. Whip the cream until stiff, fold into the avocado purée. Season with salt, pepper and brandy, if liked.

4. Fill the skins with the avocado cream. Garnish with lime zest and red peppercorns, if liked.

Tip
The avocado cream can also be seasoned with lemon juice and sprinkled with chopped chives or finely diced spring onion.

Stuffed tomatoes

Serves 4:
4 firm tomatoes
1 tin tuna fish in brine (drained weight 150 g/6 oz)
2 spring onions
1 small red pepper
100 g/4 oz mascarpone
2 tbsps cream
salt
freshly ground white pepper

Approx. 700 kJ/170 kcal per person

Preparation time: approx. 25 minutes

1. Wash the tomatoes, cut in half, and cut round the edge of each half in a zig-zag pattern. Carefully scoop out the flesh. Take the tuna fish out of the tin and drain.

2. Wash the spring onions, reserve a few green leaves for garnish, then chop the rest into very small dice. Wash the pepper, slice in half, remove the core. Finely dice one half, reserve the other for decoration.

3. Mash together the mascarpone and tuna fish to make a smooth paste, stir in the finely diced vegetables and cream. Season with salt and pepper.

4. Fill the prepared tomatoes with the tuna fish paste. Slice the reserved spring onions and pepper into strips. Use to decorate the tomatoes.

Chillies
Mix 100 g/4 oz boiled rice with 1 tbsp chopped herbs. Wash 1 fresh red and 1 green chilli, cut off the stalks and remove seeds. Stuff with herb rice.

Cherry tomatoes
Wash the tomatoes, cut off a lid and scrape out flesh using a teaspoon. Fill with scrambled egg and sprinkle with chopped chives.

Cucumber
Wash the cucumber, slice in half lengthways and scoop out flesh with a spoon. Fill with cream cheese, put 2 halves back together again and cut into slices.

Courgettes
Wash 4 courgettes, slice in half and remove flesh with a knife. Finely chop the flesh and 1 onion, fry in a little oil, then add 3 tbsps breadcrumbs and 1 bunch chopped parsley. Stuff courgettes with breadcrumb mixture. Sprinkle with parmesan and bake in the top of a preheated oven at 220° C/425°F/Gas mark 7 for about 10 minutes until brown.

Artichokes
Using a pointed knife, remove the inner leaves and the beard from 4 cooked artichokes. Melt 100 g/4 oz cream together with 100 g/4 oz gruyère cheese, then add 50 g/2 oz finely chopped ham. Fill the artichokes with the cheese mixture. Cook for about 5 minutes in a hot oven until cheese bubbles and turns brown.

Pears
Peel the pears and slice in half. Mix a little water in a pan with lemon juice. Add the pears to the pan and poach for about 5 minutes. Mix gorgonzola (or Stilton) with ground walnuts and use to fill the pear halves. May be baked in the top of the oven for about 3 minutes at 220° C/425°F/Gas mark 7 until golden brown, if liked.

Apples
Wash the apples, cut off a lid and remove the core using an apple corer. Remove some of the apple flesh with a melon baller or Parisian scoop. Sprinkle apple flesh with lemon juice. Whisk an egg white together with a little caster sugar, and mix with ground almonds, raisins and the apple flesh. Fill the hollowed-out apple with the egg mixture and bake in the centre of the oven for about 20 minutes at 220° C/425°F/Gas mark 7.

Crêpes

With a bit of practice you will soon perfect the art of making these wafer-thin pancakes. You can use whatever filling you like, because crêpes taste just as good filled with vegetables, meat or cheese as they do with fruit or sweetened cream.

Makes 12 crêpes:
250 g/9 oz plain flour
250 ml/8 fl. oz milk
125 ml/4 fl. oz water
4 eggs
salt
freshly ground white pepper
3-4 tbsps oil

Approx. 630 kJ/150 kcal per crêpe

Preparation time: approx. 35 minutes

1. Mix together the flour, water, milk and eggs to form a smooth batter. Season with salt and pepper. Leave the batter to rest for about 15 minutes.

2. To make the crêpes, heat a little oil in a non-stick pan. Spread 1-2 tbsps batter thinly across the base of the pan for each crêpe. Cook for about 1 minute on each side. Cover and keep warm until needed.

Crêpes with vegetable filling

Serves 4:
1 basic quantity crêpe batter
200 g/7 oz carrots
200 g/7 oz leeks
200 g/7 oz celery
2 tbsps butter
1 tbsp white wine (or vegetable stock)
salt
freshly ground white pepper

Approx. 2170 kJ/517 kcal per person

Preparation time: approx. 50 minutes

1. Prepare the crêpes as described in the basic recipe and keep warm.

2. Wash and clean the vegetables and cut into matchstick-sized strips.

3. Melt the butter in a pan, add the vegetables, sweat the vegetables for a little while, then glaze with the white wine. Simmer on a low heat for about 5 minutes. Season to taste with salt and pepper.

4. Shape the crêpes into cornets and fill with the prepared vegetables.

Tip
The crêpes look very decorative if filled with vegetable balls. Using a Solferino scoop, scoop balls out of vegetables such as carrots, kohlrabi and fennel; fry gently until soft and use to fill the crêpes.

Soups

Soup is an advertisement for your culinary skills, whether served as a starter, in between other courses or on its own. Soup will always go down well with guests and definitely should not be boring. Unusual ingredients, clever herb garnishes or a crispy lid will take care of this problem.

Consommé with egg garnish

Serves 4:
500 g/1 lb 2 oz stewing meat
a few bones for soup
2 bunches vegetables and herbs (e.g. carrots, leek, celery, parsley, thyme)
2 onions
150 g/6 oz frozen spinach
1 tsp white peppercorns
1 pinch nutmeg
salt
250 ml/8 fl. oz milk
4 eggs
1 tbsp tomato purée
pinch saffron (or turmeric)
3 freezer bags

Approx. 690 kJ/160 kcal per person

Preparation time: approx. 1 hour
(+ 1½ hours cooking time)

1. Quickly rinse the meat and bones. Wash and coarsely chop the vegetables. Peel the onions and cut in half. Defrost the spinach.

2. Put the meat, bones, vegetables, peppercorns, nutmeg and salt in a pan. Cover with cold water, bring to the boil and simmer gently for about 1½ hours.

3. Leave the stock to cool a little, then remove the meat and bones and pass the stock through a fine sieve. Purée the spinach.

4. To make the egg garnish, beat together the eggs and milk with a little salt. Mix ⅓ of egg with the spinach, ⅓ with tomato purée, and remaining ⅓ with saffron. Put each mixture into a separate freezer bag and fasten bag with a knot, making sure bag is airtight.

5. Simmer the bags in boiling water for about 25 minutes. Remove and leave to cool completely. Carefully cut open the bags, take out the egg mixture and cut out pretty shapes, or dice. Heat the consommé, season again, serve and decorate with egg shapes.

Crusted oxtail soup

Serves 4:
600 g/1 lb 5 oz oxtail
salt
1 bunch vegetables for soup
1 large onion
2 tbsps oil
250 ml/8 fl. oz red wine
1 bay leaf
1 sprig thyme
1 tsp black peppercorns
4 ml/approx. 1 fl. oz sherry if wished
pepper
4 packets frozen puff pastry
2 egg yolks
1 tbsp milk
For the work surface:
flour

Approx. 2200 kJ/520 kcal per person
Preparation time: approx. 40 minutes
(+ 2½ hours cooking time)

1. Cut the meat into chunks, wash, pat dry and rub with salt. Wash and coarsely chop the vegetables, peel and dice the onion.

2. Heat the oil in a saucepan and seal the meat. Add the diced vegetables and fry briefly to seal. Add 1.5 l/2½ pints water and the wine. Add the bay leaf, thyme and peppercorns to the stock. Cover, bring to boil and simmer gently for about 2½ hours.

3. Pass the stock through a fine sieve, if necessary strain off fat (page 16). Remove meat from bones, chop into small pieces and return to the stock. Season with sherry, salt and pepper.

4. Defrost the puff pastry. Beat together the egg yolks and milk and put to one side. Put the soup into 4 heat-resistant soup bowls. Preheat the oven to 220° C/425°F/Gas mark 7.

5. Roll out the puff pastry on a lightly floured work surface. Cut out 4 circles, slightly larger than the soup bowls. Brush the edges of the bowls with water, lay the pastry circles on top of the bowls, taking care not to stretch the pastry too tightly, and press down well. Using the remaining pastry, make a lattice pattern on top of the pastry lids. Brush with beaten egg and milk, and bake in the centre of the oven for about 15 minutes.

Home-made noodles or pancakes are an ideal garnish. They are rather time consuming to make, but are certainly worth the effort.

What else can garnish soup?

• Carrots, leeks and celery, cut into thin strips

• Wafer-thin slices of pecorino cheese

• Roasted peanuts

• Okra (ladies' fingers) sliced and quickly sautéed in butter

• Fine strips of fennel and beetroot, steamed for about 2 minutes

• Slices of beef marrow, warmed in the soup for about 4 minutes

• Fresh cress, chopped directly onto the soup using a pair of scissors

• Endive chopped into ribbons

• Sliced mushrooms and chopped chives

• Strips of leek made from the blanched green parts of 2 leeks (page 76)

Home-made noodles

Serves 4:
400 g/14 oz flour
4 eggs
½ tsp salt
For the work surface:
flour

Basic recipe

Approx. 1900kJ/450 kcal per person

Preparation time: approx. 40 minutes

1. Put the flour in a mixing bowl. Make a well in the centre, break the eggs into the well and add the salt. Using your hands, quickly knead to form a smooth dough. Put the dough into a plastic bag and leave to rest for about 20 minutes.

2. Divide the dough into 4 portions, and, using a noodle-making machine or a rolling pin, roll out to approx. 2 mm/$\frac{1}{10}$ inch thick. Then proceed as wished.

• Place basil leaves on half of the dough, fold over the other half and roll out again. Using a cutter, cut out small butterflies or other shapes. Cook in plenty of boiling salted water for about 5 minutes, or until *al dente*.

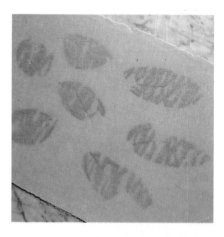

• Cut letters of the alphabet out of the dough and cook in boiling salted water.

• Place washed parsley leaves on the sheet of pastry, fold over the other half of the pastry and roll out again. Then cut into thin strips and cook in boiling salted water.

Pancake cornets

Serves 4:
100 g/4 oz flour
250 ml/8 fl. oz milk
2 eggs
salt
2 tbsps oil
chives

Approx. 960 kJ/230 kcal per person

Preparation time: approx. 30 minutes

1. Mix together flour, milk, eggs and salt. Leave to rest for 10 minutes.

2. Heat a little oil in a frying pan. Cook small pancakes, about 10 cm/4 inches in diameter, for 1 minute on each side. Add more oil to pan as required until pancake batter is used up.

3. Shape each pancake into a cornet and tie up with chives.

Variations:
Pancake rolls
Spread butter on the pancakes, roll up and cut into strips.

Pancake butterflies
Pinch the pancakes together in the middle and tie up with chives so that they look like butterflies.

Pancake gateau
Spread herb butter onto the cooled pancakes, and layer together. Wrap in cling film and weigh down with a heavy bread board or chopping board. Refrigerate for a little while. Cut into cake slices and place in soup.

Even soups which are quick and easy to make can be presented in an attractive manner.

Cream of potato soup

Serves 4:
750 g/1 lb 11 oz floury potatoes
2 onions
50 g/2 oz streaky bacon
2 tbsps butter
750 ml/1½ pints meat stock
salt
freshly ground white pepper
fresh marjoram
1 large waxy potato
1 tbsp oil
150 g/6 oz cream

Approx. 1800 kJ/430 kcal per person

Preparation time: approx. 40 minutes

1. Wash, peel and dice the floury potatoes. Peel the onions and slice into rings. Finely dice the bacon.

2. Heat the butter in a saucepan. Fry the bacon and onion rings in the butter. Gradually add the diced potato and fry. Add the stock, season with salt, pepper and marjoram. Cover and simmer for about 40 minutes.

3. In the meantime, peel the waxy potato and grate finely. Press out the liquid in a kitchen towel. Heat the oil in a small frying pan, and fry the grated potato until crisp and brown to make rosti. Drain on absorbent kitchen paper.

4. Whip the cream until it stands in soft peaks, but is not very stiff. Purée the soup and pass through a sieve if necessary. Fold in the whipped cream.

5. Fill a soup tureen or soup cups with the potato soup. Decorate with rosti and marjoram.

Tip
Instead of rosti you could also use thin, deep-fried slices of potato.

Cream of carrot soup

Serves 4:
1 kg/2 lb 3 oz carrots with tops
2 tbsps butter
750 ml/1½ pints vegetable stock
salt
sugar
½ tsp curry powder
lemon pepper
20 g/1 oz sesame seeds
100 g/4 oz double cream

Approx. 1000 kJ/250 kcal per person

Preparation time: approx. 40 minutes

1. Wash and clean the carrots, and peel if necessary. Reserve the carrot tops for garnish. Finely dice the carrots.

2. Heat the butter. Fry about 2 tbsps diced carrots for a few minutes and reserve for garnish. Fry the remaining carrots to seal, add the vegetable stock, and season with salt, sugar, curry and lemon pepper. Simmer for about 25 minutes.

3. Meanwhile roast the sesame seeds in a frying pan, without fat.

4. Purée the soup until very smooth, adjust seasoning to taste. Fold in the double cream.

5. Pour the soup into bowls. Garnish with sesame seeds, diced carrots and carrot fronds.

Cream of herb soup

Serves 4:
3 bunches mixed herbs (e.g. parsley, dill or chervil)
200 g/7 oz cream
2 tbsps butter or oil
1 tbsp flour
750 ml/1¼ pints vegetable stock (from cube)
salt
freshly ground pepper

Approx. 960 kJ/230 kcal per person

Preparation time: approx. 20 minutes

1. Wash the herbs, shake dry and chop finely. Whip the cream until stiff, mix half of the cream with 1 tbsp chopped herbs.

2. Put herb cream into a piping bag with a star-shaped nozzle, and pipe small rosettes onto a plate. Keep in the freezer until you are ready to serve the soup.

3. Heat the butter or oil in a saucepan, sprinkle the flour onto the fat, and stir in to form a roux. Gradually add half the vegetable stock, stirring all the time, add the remaining herbs and simmer for about 10 minutes.

4. Purée the soup, add the remaining vegetable stock and cream. Season with salt and pepper.

5. Pour the soup into bowls and garnish with the cream rosettes.

Cream of veal soup

Serves 4:
3 tbsps butter
2 tbsps flour
750 ml/1¼ pints ready-made veal stock
2 okra pods
250 g/9 oz cream
2 egg yolks
salt
freshly ground white pepper

Approx. 1400 kJ/330 kcal per person

Preparation time: approx. 15 minutes

1. Heat 2 tbsps butter in a pan, add the flour, and stir well to make a roux. Pour in the veal stock, stirring all the time. There shouldn't be any lumps. Simmer the soup for about 1 minute.

2. Wash the okra, dry thoroughly and cut into slices. Heat the remaining butter and toss the sliced okra in the butter.

3. Remove the soup from the heat. Beat together the cream and egg yolks and stir into the soup. Season with salt and pepper.

4. Pour the soup into bowls and garnish with okra slices.

Tip
You could use fresh mushrooms as a garnish instead of the okra.

Cream of tomato soup

Serves 4:
1 onion
1 kg/2 lb 3 oz ripe tomatoes
2 tbsps oil
500 ml/16 fl. oz meat stock (from cube)
1 sprig rosemary
salt
pepper
sugar
Tabasco sauce
12 cherry tomatoes
200 g/7 oz mozzarella cheese
1 bunch basil

Approx. 1100 kJ/260 kcal per person

Preparation time: approx. 45 minutes

1. Peel the onions and dice. Wash the tomatoes, halve, remove stalks and dice.

2. Heat the oil in a saucepan, add the tomatoes and onions and fry. Stir in the stock and add the rosemary. Season to taste with salt, pepper, sugar and Tabasco. Simmer for about 20 minutes, or until the tomatoes are soft.

3. Pass the soup through a sieve, return to the pan, and heat through. Preheat the oven to 225° C/425°F/Gas mark 7.

4. Wash the cherry tomatoes and slice. Cut out pieces of mozzarella to match the size of the tomatoes and lay on top of the slices of tomato. Bake the mozzarella slices in the top of the oven until the cheese melts and starts to brown.

5. Meanwhile wash the basil, shake dry and remove leaves from stalks. Serve the soup in bowls, float the tomato and mozzarella slices in it and garnish with basil leaves.

Cream of fish soup

Serves 4:
1 block frozen puff pastry
300 g/11 oz cod fillet
juice of 1 lemon
1 bunch spring onions
300 g/11 oz potatoes
30 g/1 oz butter
400 ml/14 fl. oz ready-made fish stock
salt
pepper
pinch saffron
100 g/4 oz crème fraiche
1 bunch dill
1-2 tbsps trout roe
For the work surface:
flour

Approx. 1500 kJ/360 kcal per person

Preparation time: approx. 50 minutes

1. Defrost the puff pastry. Preheat the oven to 220° C/425°F/Gas mark 7. Marinate the cod fillet in the lemon juice.

2. Roll out the pastry on a floured work surface and, using a small fish-shaped cutter, cut out pastry fish. Bake in the centre of the oven for about 10 minutes until golden brown.

3. Wash and finely chop the spring onions. Peel and wash the potatoes, then cut into small dice.

4. Heat the butter in a saucepan, fry the spring onions and the potato. Add the fish stock and 400 ml/14 fl. oz water. Add the fish fillets to the soup and simmer for about 25 minutes.

5. Purée the soup and pass through a sieve. Reheat in the pan, season to taste with salt, pepper and saffron. Stir in the crème fraiche.

6. Wash and dry the dill and tear into small fronds. Serve the soup, garnished with trout roe, dill fronds and pastry fish.

Tip
Instead of fresh cod you could use a smoked fish (such as trout or mackerel).

51

Vegetables and accompaniments

Attractive presentation is particularly easy with vegetables, using the natural shapes and colours. The following pages will indicate the areas to which you should pay special attention, and provide you with many valuable tips, suggestions and ideas on different ways of presenting accompaniments such as potatoes, noodles and rice. You are bound to find an option which appeals to you.

Platters of vegetables are decorative in themselves if you pay attention to the colour scheme. Remember not to boil vegetables for too long, otherwise they lose their colour and collapse.

• Clean, wash and divide 1 small cauliflower, 500 g/1 lb 2 oz broccoli and 1 head romanesco into florets. When boiled the vegetables should retain some "bite". Arrange the vegetables attractively according to colour on a dish and season with salt. Melt 2 tbsps butter, toss the vegetables in the butter and serve.

Variation:
Prepare white, green and purple-leafed cabbage as above and arrange decoratively on a plate.

Tip
Green cabbage, purple-leafed cabbage varieties and romanesco are only available from June to November.

• Wash 400 g/14 oz each carrots, courgettes, kohlrabi and 300 g/11 oz tinned bamboo shoots; peel, and cut into even-sized thin sticks. Cook the vegetables separately in boiling water with 1 tbsp lemon juice until done but still slightly crisp. Tie up the bamboo

shoots with strips of pepper if wished. Arrange the assorted vegetables on a plate lined with chicory or spinach leaves. Sprinkle with salt and pepper. Melt 2 tbsps butter and drizzle over vegetables.

• Wash 300 g/11 oz each carrots and baby turnips, and peel thinly if necessary. Don't remove the green tops. Cook in boiling water with a drop of vinegar added to it until cooked but still crisp, then toss in melted butter. Wash 300 g/11 oz mangold (or swede). Cut the leaves into 3 cm/1 inch wide strips. Dice the vegetables. Fry briefly in a little butter, season with salt and pepper. Arrange the various vegetables on a large plate and serve.

Vegetable platter

Serves 4:
500 g/1 lb 2 oz white asparagus
500 g/1 lb 2 oz green asparagus
300 g/11 oz mangetout
1 tbsp salt
1 tsp sugar
1 tsp vinegar
1 tbsp butter
1 small courgette, if liked
a few chervil leaves, if liked
kitchen thread

Approx. 530 kJ/130 kcal per person

Preparation time: approx. 1 hour

1. Wash and remove the woody stalk ends from both types of asparagus, peel the white asparagus. Divide the asparagus into separate bundles of white and green and tie up with kitchen thread. Wash the mangetout and remove any string.

2. Heat water in a large saucepan, add the salt and sugar. Bring quickly to boil, then turn down the heat slightly. Put the white asparagus in the pan and simmer for 15 minutes or until tender. Remove from pan and keep warm. Put the green asparagus in the pan and simmer for 10 minutes, but do not let it boil. Remove from pan and keep warm.

3. Heat water in another pan with the vinegar. Add the mangetout to the pan and boil for about 5 minutes. Remove from pan and keep warm.

4. Arrange the 3 different vegetables on a large platter. Melt the butter, sprinkle over vegetables and serve. Garnish with courgette balls and chervil leaves if liked.

Carved vegetables

Serves 4:
3 carrots
1 celeriac root
3 baby turnips
1 yellow and 1 green courgette
3 tbsps butter
salt
freshly ground white pepper
chicory leaves if liked

Approx. 420 kJ/100 kcal per person

Preparation time: approx. 60 minutes

1. Wash and peel the carrots, celeriac and baby turnips, then cut into 4 cm/1½ inch long pieces. Using a vegetable knife, cut the vegetables into torpedo shapes.

2. Heat the butter in a large saucepan, add the vegetables and sweat over a low heat for about 10 minutes. The vegetables should retain their shape and colour. Season with salt and pepper.

3. Arrange the vegetables prettily on a plate, possibly on a bed of chicory leaves.

¤ The vegetables are a suitable accompaniment to fish dishes.

Tip
It takes a little practice to be able to cut the vegetables into a torpedo shape. Don't be disappointed if you don't get it spot on the first time. You can always use the left over vegetables to make a cream of vegetable soup.

Pepper ratatouille

Serves 4:
1 small firm aubergine
salt
juice of 1 lemon
2 small courgettes
1 red, 1 green and 1 yellow pepper
1 large onion
3 tbsps olive oil
1 sprig fresh rosemary
freshly ground white pepper

Approx. 530 kJ/130 kcal per person

Preparation time: approx. 60 minutes

1. Wash the aubergine and remove the stalk. Cut the aubergine into diamonds and sprinkle with salt. Leave to stand for about 10 minutes.

2. Meanwhile heat some water in a saucepan, add the lemon juice. Rinse the aubergine and blanch for about 3 minutes, remove from pan and leave to drain.

3. Wash the courgettes and peppers, remove stalks and cores, and slice the vegetables into diamond shapes. Peel the onion and slice into diamonds as well.

4. Heat the oil in a large frying pan, add the vegetables and sweat for about 5 minutes. The vegetable diamonds should retain their shape and colour.

5. Wash the rosemary, pat dry and strip needles. Sprinkle over vegetables, season with salt and pepper, and serve.

Tip
Serve the ratatouille as an accompaniment to lamb or as a light main meal with crusty French bread.

Root vegetables are particularly well suited to this type of decoration, as is any other firm-fleshed vegetable, such as carrots or celeriac.

Vegetable balls
Wash and peel carrots and a celeriac root. Using a Solferino scoop or Parisienne scoop, and applying even pressure, scoop out vegetable balls. These are suitable for a vegetable platter.

Courgette ovals
Wash a courgette and cut into chunks approx. 5 cm/2 inches long. Using a small, sharp vegetable knife, shape the chunks all round to make a rugby ball shape. A good accompaniment to meat.

Vegetable flowers
Wash carrots and courgettes, peel the carrots. Using a cannel knife, score grooves along the vegetables, then slice. Good with fish.

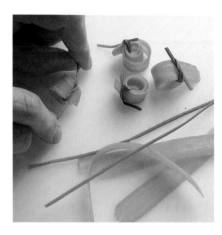

Carrot curls
Peel a fresh carrot and cut off the root. Using a vegetable peeler, peel off long, wafer-thin strips. Roll up the strips of carrot into curls and secure with chives. A pretty decoration for meat and fish dishes.

Vegetable shapes
Cut carrots or celeriac into long slices. Use decorative cutters to cut out pretty shapes. Particularly attractive as a garnish for soups.

Stuffed courgette flowers

Makes 9 flowers:
250 g/9 oz sole fillets
salt
lemon pepper
1 morel mushroom
1 egg white
150 g/6 oz cream
1 courgette
9 courgette flowers
400 ml/14 fl. oz fish stock

Approx. 350 kJ/83 kcal per person

Preparation time: approx. 1 hour

1. Chop the sole into small dice, season with salt and pepper and leave to marinate for about 15 minutes in the refrigerator. Soften the morel in water for about 20 minutes.

2. Purée the fish in a blender or food processor with the egg white. Whip the cream until it stands in soft peaks and fold into the fish. Refrigerate.

The pistils in the courgette flowers are best removed with a small, pointed kitchen knife.

3. Wash the courgettes and dice very finely. Remove the morel from the water and dice finely. Divide the fish purée into 3 portions. Mix ⅓ with the diced courgette, and ⅓ with the morel. Leave the final portion without any addition.

It is very easy to stuff the flowers using a piping bag with a large round nozzle.

4. Carefully wash the courgette flowers and pat dry. Remove the pistil. Fill 3 blossoms each with the different fillings. Carefully pull the petals together to enclose the filling.

5. Heat the fish stock in a saucepan with 300 ml/½ pint water. Simmer the courgette flowers in the stock for about 3 minutes. Remove and serve while lukewarm.

¤ Goes well with crusty French bread.

Tip
You can use fillets of plaice or flounder instead of sole. The courgette flowers can also be stuffed with veal or chicken forcemeat.

Baked stuffed vegetables

Whether as a tasty snack or an attractive introduction to a meal, stuffed vegetables are a culinary treat well suited to any occasion.

Tomatoes au gratin

Serves 4:
4 large tomatoes
300 g/11 oz spinach
salt
freshly grated nutmeg
1 tbsp oil
pepper
1 egg white
30 g/1 oz freshly grated parmesan

Approx. 440 kJ/100 kcal per person

Preparation time: approx. 30 minutes

1. Wash the tomatoes, cut off a lid and remove the flesh.

2. Wash and clean the spinach, cut off the large stalks. Blanch for about 1 minute in salted water and rinse in ice-cold water. Drain the spinach, season with salt and nutmeg and toss in 1 tbsp oil.

3. Season the inside of the tomatoes with salt and pepper. Fill with spinach and brush outside of tomatoes with remaining oil.

4. Preheat the oven to 200°C/400°F/ Gas mark 6. Whisk the egg white with a pinch of salt until stiff, fold in the parmesan. Put the egg mixture in a piping bag with a star-shaped nozzle and pipe around the edge of the tomatoes.

5. Bake the tomatoes in the top of the oven for about 10 minutes.

¤ Especially good as an accompaniment to meat dishes.

Stuffed aubergines

Serves 4:
300 g/11 oz floury potatoes
1 egg yolk
100 ml/4 fl. oz milk
freshly grated nutmeg
salt
2 medium-sized aubergines
200 g/7 oz lamb
10 pitted black olives
2 sprigs fresh thyme (or dried)
3 tbsps oil
freshly ground white pepper

Approx. 1100 kJ/260 kcal per person

Preparation time: approx. 1½ hours

1. Wash the potatoes, put in a pan with enough water to cover and simmer for about 20 minutes. Leave to cool a little, remove skins, and press through a potato ricer into a bowl or mash using a potato masher. Preheat the oven to 220° C/Gas mark 6.

2. Add the egg yolk and the milk to the potato, season with salt and nutmeg and combine thoroughly.

3. Cut the aubergines in half. Sprinkle salt on the cut surfaces. Leave for 20 minutes.

4. Meanwhile cut the lamb into thin strips. Halve the olives, wash the thyme, shake dry and remove leaves. Marinate the meat for 10 minutes in 1 tbsp oil and half of the thyme.

5. Heat 1 tbsp oil in a pan, fry the meat for about 2 minutes. Add the olives, season with salt and pepper.

6. Line a baking sheet with baking parchment and brush with remaining oil. Drain the aubergines on kitchen paper, lay cut surface down on the baking sheet. Bake in the centre of the oven for about 20 minutes. Remove from oven and, using a spoon, scrape out the flesh.

7. Put the mashed potato in a piping bag with a large round nozzle. Fill the

aubergine halves with the meat and olives; decorate with piped mashed potato and bake for about 10 minutes until potato browns. Garnish with remaining thyme.

Tip
You can also use instant mashed potato.

Delicious potatoes

Potatoes are a flexible side dish which can be prepared in almost 1001 ways. They go well with meat, fish and poultry.

Mashed potato

Serves 4:
1 kg/2 lb 3 oz floury potatoes
250 ml/8 fl. oz milk
60 g/2 oz butter
salt
freshly grated nutmeg

Basic recipe

Approx. 1400 kJ/330 kcal per person

Preparation time: approx. 40 minutes

1. Wash and peel the potatoes and cut into quarters. Cover with salted water, bring to boil and cook for about 20 minutes, until tender. Discard the water and mash the potatoes.

2. Gently heat the butter and milk and add to mashed potato. Using a balloon whisk, beat to a light, fluffy purée, then season with salt and nutmeg.

Variations:
Red and green mashed potato
It looks very pretty when portions of the mashed potato are different colours. Divide the prepared mashed potato in half. Mix half with 1 tbsp tomato purée, and the other with 1 tbsp chopped herbs. Put mashed potato in a piping bag with a round or star-shaped nozzle and pipe out shapes as required.

Potato rosettes (Duchesse potatoes)
Preheat the oven to 220° C/425°F/Gas mark 7. Beat 2 egg yolks into the prepared mashed potato. Put the mashed potato in a piping bag with a large star-shaped nozzle, and pipe potato rosettes onto a baking sheet lined with baking parchment. Bake until golden brown.

Tip
You can also used instant mashed potato.

Potato nests

Makes 4 nests:
500 g/1 lb 2 oz floury potatoes
For deep frying:
Oil
Special double sieve
(or 1 large and 1 small sieve)

Approx. 820 kJ/200 kcal per nest

Preparation time: approx. 30 minutes

1. Peel the potatoes, cut into

matchsticks or wafer-thin slices. Dry
well on a tea towel.

2. Heat the oil until very hot in a small

deep-sided pan. Brush the large sieve
with oil, line with ¼ of the potatoes,
and press down the small sieve inside
the large one, on top of the potatoes.
Fry for approx. 5 minutes in the hot oil
until golden brown.

3. Remove the sieve, place on kitchen
paper and open up. Carefully remove
the potato nest. Keep warm. Fry the
remaining 3 nests in the same way.

4. Fill the baskets with your choice of
cooked vegetables or salad.

Tip
As an accompaniment to lamb, fill the
potato baskets with dwarf beans.

Peeled, raw potatoes can be cut into
many different shapes and then boiled
or fried.
• Make potato balls (pommes
Parisienne) with a scoop
• Cut out potato lattices using a
serrated knife
• Slice, turning 90° each time so that a
lattice pattern is formed.
• Julienne strips
• Matchstick-sized strips
• Different-sized dice
• Slices of different thicknesses
• Torpedo shapes using a vegetable
knife

Potato waffles

Makes 12 waffles:
400 g/14 oz floury potatoes
50 g/2 oz butter
150 g/6 oz crème fraiche
250 ml/8. fl. oz milk
approx. 20 g/1 oz yeast
200 g/7 oz flour
salt
freshly grated nutmeg
3 eggs
For the waffle iron:
3 tbsps oil

Approx. 940 kJ/220 kcal per waffle

Preparation time: approx. 1½ hours

1. Wash the potatoes and cook in a little salted water for about 20 minutes until tender. Leave until steam has evaporated, remove skins whilst still hot, and grate finely.

2. Stir the butter and crème fraiche into the potatoes.

3. Gently heat the milk, dissolve the yeast in it and mix to a smooth paste with the flour. Add to the potato mixture, season with salt and nutmeg. Cover the potato mixture and leave to work for about 35 minutes.

4. Stir the eggs into the potato mixture. Heat the waffle iron, brush with oil, and bake waffles until crisp.

Tip
You can adapt the taste of the waffles using ground nuts or finely chopped herbs.

Potato cakes

Serves 4:
500 g/1 lb 2 oz floury potatoes
1 egg
60 g/2 oz flour
salt
freshly ground black pepper
3 tbsps clarified butter

Basic recipe

Approx. 930 kJ/220 kcal per person

Preparation time: approx. 1 hour

1. Wash the potatoes and cook in a little water for 30 minutes until tender.

Allow steam to evaporate, remove skins whilst still hot and mash or push through a potato ricer. Leave to cool.

2. Stir the egg, flour, salt and pepper into the potato. The mixture must be stiff. If necessary, add a little more flour.

3. Shape a roll approx. 5 cm/2 inches in diameter out of mashed potato. Using a floured knife, slice the roll into finger-thick slices.

4. Heat the clarified butter in a frying pan, and cook the potato cakes for about 3 minutes on each side until golden brown.

Tip
You can adapt the basic recipe as you

wish. You can add chopped parsley or fried diced bacon to the mashed potato. Or you can roast ground hazelnuts in a pan and mix them into the potato.

Variations:
Quenelles
Shape the mashed potato into finger-thick quenelles and fry in the hot clarified butter.

Gnocchi
Make a finger-thick sausage out of mashed potato. Cut the sausage into 3 cm/1¼-inch slices, and press down on each slice with the prongs of a fork to form a pattern. Cook the gnocci in salted water at a rolling boil for about 10 minutes.

A new outlook on noodles

Noodles not only go well in soups (page 46), they are also good with meat and fish, or in a sauce as a main dish in their own right. The advantage of noodles is that they are quick to make and can be adapted in many ways.

Noodle nests

Makes 4 nests:
500 g / 1 lb 2 oz Chinese egg noodles
For deep frying:
oil
special double sieve
(or 1 large and 1 small sieve)

1. Cook the egg noodles in plenty of boiling salted water until soft, but still *al dente*. Rinse in cold water. Dry thoroughly.

2. Heat the oil in a large saucepan. Line the large sieve with ¼ of the noodles, press the small sieve down into the noodles.

3. Fry the nest in the hot oil for about 3 minutes until crisp and brown.

4. Carefully remove the noodle nest. Keep warm. Fry the remaining 3 nests in the same way.

5. Fill with ragout, meat sauce or seafood as preferred.

Noodle nests

Herb noodles

Saffron noodles

Variations:
Beetroot noodles
200 ml/6 fl. oz beetroot juice
1 quantity basic noodle dough (see page 46)

Reduce beetroot juice to half and leave to cool. Mix with eggs used in basic recipe and add to noodle mixture.

Herb noodles
3 tbsps mixed chopped herbs
1 quantity basic noodle dough (page 46)

Mix the herbs with the eggs used in the basic recipe. Prepare the noodle dough according to the basic recipe.

Saffron noodles
1 tsp saffron (or turmeric)
1 quantity basic noodle dough (page 46)

Dissolve the saffron in 2 tbsps hot water. Mix with the eggs used in the basic recipe. Prepare the noodle dough according to the basic recipe.

Salmon lasagne

Serves 4:
4 sheets of lasagne from a packet
100 g/4 oz mascarpone
100 g/4 oz pecorino cheese, freshly grated
100 g/4 oz spinach
4 slices smoked salmon
1 bunch dill

Approx. 1200 kJ/290 kcal per person

Preparation time: approx. 45 minutes

1. Cook the sheets of lasagne according to the instructions on the packet and cut in half.

2. Mix together the mascarpone and pecorino cheeses. Preheat the oven to 220° C/425°F/Gas mark 7.

3. Clean the spinach, wash and blanch for 1 minute in boiling water. Rinse under cold water. Leave to dry thoroughly on a tea towel.

4. Make each serving by putting ½ a sheet of lasagne on a baking plate. Spread mascarpone over the lasagne. Divide spinach amongst servings of lasagne. Place a slice of smoked salmon and ½ a sheet of lasagne on top. Spread mascarpone on top of the lasagne. The layers should be clearly visible.

5. Bake the lasagne in the centre of the oven for about 8 minutes, until the

cheese melts. In the meantime wash the dill, dry and chop coarsely. Garnish the lasagne with dill.

Tip
You can use sorrel leaves instead of spinach.

Variation:
Lasagne with shiitake mushrooms
Use a vegetarian filling for the lasagne. Finely chop 100 g/4 oz shiitake mushrooms and 2 spring onions. Fry in a little olive oil and season with salt, pepper, nutmeg and soy sauce. Mix 100 g/4 oz crème fraiche with 50 g/2 oz grated hard cheese and 1 bunch chopped parsley and layer alternately with the lasagne. The top layer should be cheese mixture. Bake for about 8 minutes.

Shaped and coloured rice

Rice is great for moulding into different shapes, using all kinds of containers such as timbales, savarin moulds, jelly moulds and so on. Or you can simply use cups or a loaf tin in which different coloured rice is layered together and then turned out. Rice is a versatile accompaniment, which can be coloured to match the main dish. All quantities given are for 4 people. Plain rice contains about 910 kJ/220 kcal per portion.

Wild rice

150 g/6 oz wild rice
1 tbsp butter
500 ml/16 fl. oz stock
salt

Rinse and drain the rice. Heat the butter in a pan, brown the rice in the butter. Add the stock to the rice, season with salt, cover and simmer on a low heat for about 50 minutes

Tomato rice

500 ml/16 fl. oz tomato juice
Tabasco sauce
250 g/9 oz long grain rice
1 tbsp oil
4 individual moulds

Put the tomato juice in a pan, season with a dash of Tabasco and bring to boil. Rinse the rice, add to the tomato juice, bring quickly to boil, turn off the heat, cover and leave to swell for 25 minutes. Brush the moulds with oil, fill with rice, pressing down firmly and turn out onto plates.

Spinach rice

100 g/4 oz frozen spinach
1 tbsp butter
500 ml/16 fl. oz vegetable stock
250 g/9 oz long grain rice
1 tbsp oil
4 individual moulds

Defrost the spinach. Heat the butter in a pan, add the spinach and fry for about 1 minute until soft. Purée in a blender or food processor. Return the spinach to the pan, add the stock and bring to boil. Rinse the rice, add to the spinach, cover and simmer for 25 minutes. Grease the moulds with oil, fill with warm rice, pressing down firmly, and turn out onto plates.

Beetroot rice

500 ml/16 fl. oz beetroot juice
250 g/9 oz long grain rice
1 tbsp oil
4 individual moulds

Bring the beetroot juice to the boil in a
pan. Rinse the rice and add to the
boiling juice. Turn off the heat, cover,
and leave to swell for 25 minutes.
Brush the moulds with oil. Fill with
the warm rice, pressing down firmly.
Turn out onto plates.

Saffron rice

500 ml/16 fl. oz vegetable stock (from
cube)
1 jar saffron
250 g/9 oz long grain rice
1 tbsp oil

Bring the vegetable stock to the boil
with the saffron powder in a pan.
Rinse the rice, add to the stock, turn
off the heat, cover and leave for 25
minutes. Brush the moulds with oil,
fill with still warm rice, pressing down
firmly. Turn out onto plates.

Carrot rice

500 ml/16 fl. oz carrot juice
½ tsp curry powder
250 g/9 oz long grain rice
1 tbsp oil
4 individual moulds

Bring the carrot juice to the boil with
the curry powder. Rinse the rice, add
to the carrot juice and bring quickly to
the boil. Turn off the heat, cover and
leave for about 25 minutes. Brush the
moulds with the oil, fill with warm
rice, pressing down firmly. Turn out
onto plates.

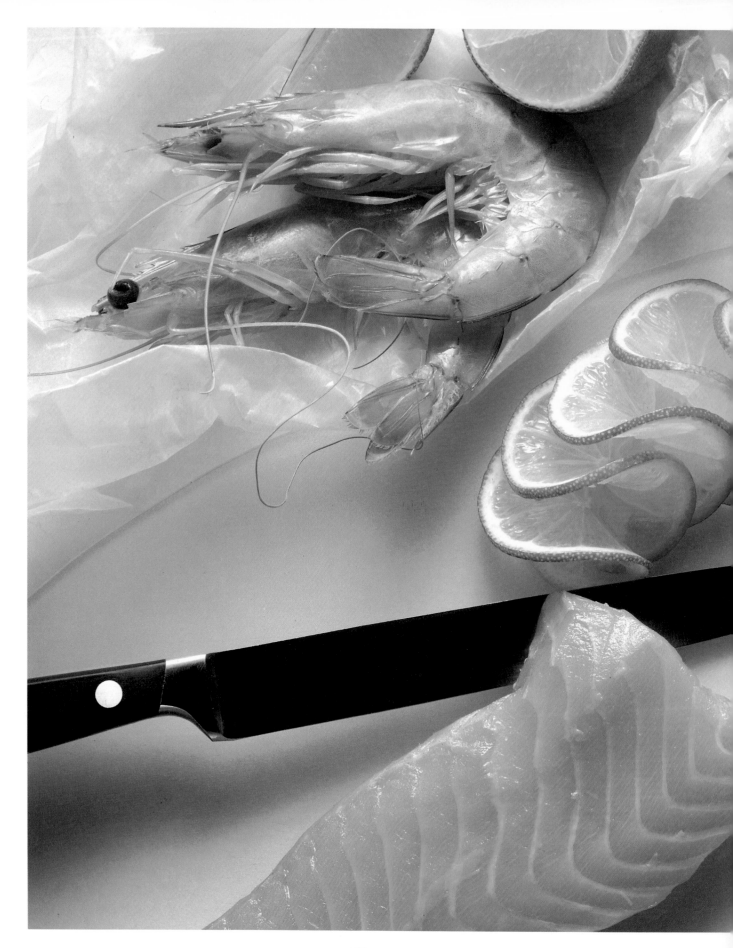

Fish and seafood

Why don't you try out one of the suggestions in the following chapter – it is packed with a wide variety of recipes and as you will see, you don't need too much inspiration to serve fish and seafood in new and interesting ways.

Even if you were to serve this fish dish three times running, you would still be able to surprise your guests every time. The secret is in the presentation. Here is the recipe, with several different serving options.

Variation:
Star fish

Cut the salmon into strips. These should be the same size as the fillets of sole. Prepare the dish according to the basic recipe. Divide the sauce between 4 plates, arrange the 2 types of fish in the shape of a star fish.

Fish plait

Cut the sole fillets in half lengthways, plait in a strip of salmon and secure

each end with a toothpick. Prepare the dish as described in the basic recipe. Arrange the plait with the sauce.

Tip
Instead of sole fillets you can use plaice or flounder.

Decorate the fillets with strips of green leek or spring onions. Simmer the vegetable strips briefly in the fish stock and arrange with the fish.

Fish rope

This is a particularly attractive way to present boiled fish.

Serves 4:
8 fillets of sole (approx. 500 g)/approx. 1 lb 2 oz
400 g/11 oz salmon fillet
1 tbsp lemon juice
3 shallots
1 tbsp butter
200 ml/7 fl. oz fish stock
250 ml/8 fl. oz white wine
200 g/7 oz double cream
1 pinch saffron
salt
freshly ground white pepper
1 bunch dill
toothpicks

Basic recipe

Approx. 2600 kJ/620 kcal per person

Preparation time: approx. 30 minutes

1. Slice the sole fillets in half lengthways. Cut the salmon fillet into strips. The salmon strips should be the same length as the fillets of sole. Drizzle with lemon juice. Twist together 1 strip of sole and 1 of salmon to form a rope. Secure the ends with a toothpick.

2. Peel the shallots and dice finely. Heat the butter in a saucepan, fry the shallots in the butter for about 2 minutes. Pour in the fish stock and white wine and simmer for about 5 minutes.

3. Carefully place the fish ropes in the stock and cook for about 6 minutes. Remove from pan, cover and keep warm.

4. Stir in the double cream and saffron and reduce the sauce until thick. Season with salt and pepper.

5. Wash the dill, dry and chop finely, reserving a few fronds for garnish. Add the chopped dill to the fish sauce.

6. Arrange the fish ropes decoratively on a plate, remove the toothpicks if desired and pour sauce over fish. Garnish with dill fronds.

▪ Goes with wild rice.

Fish rolls make a tasty starter or go well with noodles as a main course. You can make fish rolls with almost any type of vegetable.

Plaice rolls with spinach

Serves 4:
100 g/4 oz frozen leaf spinach
8 plaice fillets (about 500 g)/about 1 lb 2 oz
2 tbsps lemon juice
salt
freshly ground white pepper
400 ml/14 fl. oz fish stock
125 ml/4 fl. oz white wine
100 g/4 oz cream
toothpicks if needed

Basic recipe

Approx. 870 kJ/210 kcal per person

Preparation time: approx. 30 minutes

1. Defrost the spinach and blanch quickly in boiling water. Then rinse in cold water and spread the leaves on a tea towel or kitchen paper.

2. Spread out the plaice fillets on a board. Drizzle lemon juice over fish, season with salt and pepper. Cut the fillets in half lengthways. Lay the spinach leaves on top of the fillets and roll up. If necessary secure with toothpicks.

3. Heat the fish stock in a saucepan with the white wine. Place the rolls in the pan and simmer for about 6 minutes. Remove the rolls, cover and keep warm. Stir the cream into the fish stock and cook at a fast boil until reduced to a thick consistency.

4. Arrange the rolls decoratively on a plate with the sauce.

■ Wild rice or thin noodles are a good accompaniment. Decorate with strips of leek.

Tip
When rolling up the fish fillets the skin side should always face inward.

Variations:
Plaice rolls with courgette
Prepare the plaice fillets as described in the basic recipe. Wash 2 small courgettes and, using a lemon zester, peel off strips of skin from 1 courgette. Then cut the courgettes lengthways into thin strips and season with salt. Roll up with the prepared fish fillets and cook as described in the basic recipe. Arrange the fish rolls on the sauce. Decorate with courgette strips.

Plaice rolls with peppers
Drain 4 red pepper halves (preserved, approx. 200 g/7 oz drained weight) and cut into strips as wide as the fish fillets. Roll up with the prepared fish fillets. Prepare the rolls as described in the basic recipe. Arrange with the sauce on a plate, garnish with 1 spring onion tassel (page 76).

Drain 4 yellow pepper halves (preserved, approx. 200 g/7 oz drained weight) and cut into strips as wide as the fish fillets. Roll up with the prepared fish fillets. Prepare the rolls as described in the basic recipe. Arrange with the sauce on a plate, garnish with slices of star fruit.

Tip
Instead of using preserved peppers, you can of course use fresh. Before using them you must remove the skin with a vegetable peeler.

The fish rolls look very decorative and colourful if the different types are arranged on a platter.

Decorations for fish

These vegetables, which can be used to make wonderful decorations for fish, are available almost all year round.

strips into a bow, wrap the third strip around the middle. Trim the ends to even them up.

Leek palms

Thoroughly wash a leek. Cut a piece approx. 15 cm/6 inches long out of the middle. Make lots of narrow cuts in the green end, but don't cut all the way through. Then place in cold water so that the palm can open out.

Spring onion tassels

Wash a spring onion and remove the roots. Cut into pieces 5 cm/2 inches long. Wash a red chilli pod and cut into rings. Remove the seeds. Push down 1 chilli ring onto each of the pieces of spring onion. Make multiple cuts in each end of the spring onion to make very thin strips. Lay the tassels in cold water so that the strips open up to give a more tasselled effect.

Courgette bundles

Wash 1 green and 1 yellow courgette, and cut into thin matchsticks approx. 10 cm/4 inches long. Tie up in a bundle with a strand of chives or the green from a spring onion.

Leek bows

Thoroughly wash a leek. Blanch the green end of the leek in boiling water and leave to cool in cold water. Cut off 3 strips 20 cm/8 inches in length and 3 cm/1 inch wide. Shape 2 of the leek

Courgette as a vegetable accompaniment

Wash a courgette, cut in half lengthways and divide into 4. Using a sharp pointed knife or a linoleum knife, cut pattern in the courgette skin. Toss quickly in butter.

Papaya slices
Peel a papaya, cut in half and remove the seeds with a spoon. Cut the flesh into thin slices.

Lime spirals
Cut a lime into thin slices, make a cut in the edge of each lime slice through to the centre. Shape each slice into a twist and arrange several twists together to make a spiral.

Lemon slices
Using a cannel knife, score deep grooves around the lemon. The grooves should be equidistant from each other. Then slice the lemon.

Star fruit
Slice a star fruit to show off the natural star shape.

Fruit slices
Using a zester, remove strips from the skins of a lemon, orange and lime. Then arrange strips of zest decoratively on top of lemon slices.

Serve this dish on particularly festive occasions, because it can be prepared well in advance. You can be enjoying an aperitif with your guests whilst the trout is cooking in the oven.

Serves 4:
1 salmon trout (gutted and cleaned, approx. 700 g)/approx. 1 lb 9 oz
1 tbsp lemon juice
salt
freshly ground white pepper
450 g/1 lb frozen puff pastry
1 bunch flat-leafed parsley
50 g/2 oz butter
1 egg yolk
2 tbsps milk
200 g/7 oz crème fraiche
1 tsp Dijon mustard
1 tsp horseradish (ready made)
For the work surface:
flour
For the baking sheet:
fat

Approx. 4000 kJ/950 kcal per person

Preparation time: approx. 1½ hours

1. Rinse the salmon trout under cold water, pat dry and drizzle lemon juice both inside and outside the fish. Season with salt and pepper.

2. Defrost the puff pastry.

3. Wash the parsley, shake dry and chop finely. Melt the butter, mix with the parsley. Brush the parsley butter on the inside and outside of the fish.

4. Preheat the oven to 200°C/400°F/ Gas mark 6. Roll out the puff pastry thinly on a lightly floured work surface. Place the salmon trout on the pastry and wrap up so that the fish is completely covered. About ¼ of the pastry should be left over to make the scales. Moisten the pastry seams with water to help them stick together. Beat together the egg yolk and milk and brush the trout with half of the egg wash.

5. Cut out circles 5 cm/2 inches in diameter from the remaining pastry and layer on the fish so they look like scales; brush with the remaining egg wash.

6. Grease a baking sheet. Carefully place the trout on the sheet and bake in the centre of the oven for about 30 minutes. The pastry should be golden brown.

7. Mix together the crème fraiche, mustard and horseradish and serve with the trout.

Tip
Ask your fishmonger to remove the backbone.

Seafood dishes look especially nice if served in the shell. The following dishes can be served as appetisers or between courses.

Scallops

Ingredients for 8 scallops
8 scallops (fresh or deep frozen)
1 tbsp lime juice
2 bunches spring onions
250 g/9 oz cream
20 ml/2 tbsps fino sherry if wished
Tabasco sauce
2 star anise seeds
salt
freshly ground white pepper
3 tbsps butter

1 lime
parsley or chives

Approx. 1200 kJ/290 kcal per person

Preparation time: approx. 45 minutes

1. Defrost frozen scallops, rinse fresh ones. Using a knife, open the scallops and carefully remove the corals. Sprinkle lemon juice over the scallops.

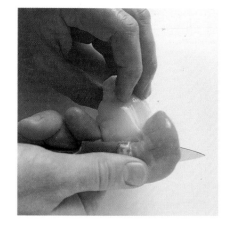

2. Finely chop the spring onions.

3. Put the cream, sherry, a dash Tabasco and star anise in a saucepan. Bring to boil and reduce to half, season with salt and pepper. Remove the star anise.

4. Melt 2 tbsps butter in a frying pan. Quickly toss the corals in the butter and remove. Add the scallops to the pan and fry for about 2 minutes. Season with salt and pepper. Add to the sauce, with the corals, for about 1 minute.

5. Wash the lime in hot water and cut into slices. Add the spring onions to the frying pan with the remaining butter and fry for about 1 minute. Arrange on the scallop shells.

6. Remove the scallops and corals from the sauce and arrange on top of the spring onions. Using a hand mixer or balloon whisk, beat the sauce. Put the scallop shells with the scallops on a plate, pour sauce over scallops. Garnish with chervil or parsley leaves and lime slices.

■ Serve with toasted slices of white bread.

Mussels

Serves 6:
2.5 kg/5½ lb mussels
5 shallots
2 carrots
2 sticks celery
4 tbsps olive oil
375 ml/12 fl. oz dry white wine
1 bay leaf
2 bunches mixed herbs (parsley, dill, mint)
2 cloves garlic
1 tbsp coarsely ground almonds
salt
freshly ground black pepper
For the dish:
fat

Approx. 900 kJ/210 kcal per person

Preparation time: approx. 45 minutes

1. Wash the mussels, scrub them and remove beards. Throw away opened mussels because they are inedible.

2. Peel and finely dice the shallots. Wash the carrots, peel and finely dice. Wash the celery and slice into small rings.

3. Heat 2 tbsps olive oil in a deep, wide pan; add the finely chopped vegetables and fry for about 3 minutes. Glaze with the wine and 250 ml/8 fl. oz water. Add the mussels and the bay leaf. Simmer until the mussels open.

4. Wash the herbs, pat dry, then chop finely. Peel the garlic cloves, chop finely or put through a garlic press and add to the herbs. Mix with the remaining oil and the almonds. Season with salt and pepper.

5. Remove the mussels from the stock and throw away any which are unopened. Break open the shells, remove the inner beard and upper half of the shell. Preheat the oven to 220° C/425°F/Gas mark 7.

6. Grease a shallow, heat-resistant dish and arrange the mussels decoratively in it. Sprinkle the herb mixture on top. Pour a little stock into the dish and bake in the centre of the oven for about 10 minutes. Serve hot.

▨ Serve with crusty French bread.

Tip
Mussels are in season from October to March. They should always be eaten fresh. Other types of shellfish such as cockles can be prepared in the same way. They are also available in tins from good grocers.

The following recipes can either be served as a starter for 4 people or a main-course dish for 2 people. Crusty white bread is a good accompaniment.

Herby prawns

Ingredients for 12 prawns:
12 fresh king prawns (without head, with tails)
1 clove garlic
1 sprig rosemary
4 tbsps cold-pressed olive oil
1 tbsp lemon juice
1 bunch basil
salt
freshly ground white pepper

Approx. 380 kJ/90 kcal per person

Preparation time: approx. 30 minutes
(+ 30 minutes marinating time)

1. Remove the prawns from their shells. Using a sharp knife, remove the dark thread along the back of the prawns.

2. Peel and finely chop the garlic. Wash the rosemary, shake dry, peel the needles from the stalk and chop them finely. Put 2 tbsps olive oil in a bowl; add the garlic, rosemary and lemon juice; and stir to form a marinade. Put the prawns in the marinade and leave to marinate for about 30 minutes.

3. Wash the basil, dry and chop coarsely. Heat the remaining olive oil. Remove the prawns from the marinade and fry for about 2 minutes in the oil. Season with salt and pepper. Remove and sprinkle with basil.

Prawns in batter

12 scampi tails (uncooked, fresh or frozen)
salt
curry powder
2 eggs
50 g/2 oz rice flour
(or ordinary flour)
3 tbsps white wine
(or water)
125 ml/4 fl. oz oil
2 limes

Approx. 740 kJ/180 kcal per scampi

Preparation time: approx. 30 minutes

1. Defrost the frozen scampi. Remove the scampi from their shells. Remove the dark thread on the back with a pointed knife. Season with salt and curry.

2. Separate the eggs. Mix the flour, wine and egg yolks together. Whisk the egg whites until stiff and fold into the batter.

3. Heat the oil in a frying pan. Dip the scampi in the batter and fry in the hot oil, turning frequently, until golden brown. Serve with slices of lime.

Tip
The prawns look especially attractive if arranged on a bed of fresh seaweed. They also look nice presented on noodle nests, herb rice, wild rice or plain boiled rice.

A wide range of large prawns is available, which go by many different names such as scampi, deep sea prawns, gambas, and king prawns.

Oriental prawns

Ingredients for 12 prawns:
12 prawns
(fresh or frozen)
1 tsp cornflour
2 tbsps soy sauce
1 tbsp sherry if required
1 tsp honey
1 chilli pod
½ tsp ground caraway
1 tsp chilli sauce
(or tomato ketchup)
3 tbsps oil

Approx. 300 kJ/71 kcal per person

Preparation time: about 30 minutes

1. Defrost the frozen prawns. Remove the prawns from their shells. Leave the tail ends on. Remove the dark thread from the back of the prawns with a sharp knife. Using kitchen paper, pat the prawns dry.

2. Mix the cornflour with the soy sauce, sherry and honey. Wash the chilli, cut in half lengthways, remove the seeds and cut the pod into small pieces. Stir into the sauce with the caraway and the chilli sauce.

3. Heat the oil in a large frying pan. Fry the prawns in the hot oil until they turn pink. Stir in the sauce and leave the prawns to simmer in the mixture for about 1 minute.

From top to bottom: herby prawns, battered prawns, Oriental prawns

Meat and poultry

The meat or poultry dish is almost always the high point of a meal. You can crown every menu by using simple techniques, in very little time. Let the following pages help you to choose suitable accompaniments or the correct carving technique, because the secret is simply knowing what to do and when to do it.

Variations:
Roast pork with pumpkin leaves
Leaves made from pumpkin are a particularly attractive decoration and accompaniment to roast meats. Peel 1 pumpkin and cut into slices. Use a chestnut leaf or vine leaf as a template and cut out leaves from the pumpkin. Blanch for approx. 1 minute in boiling water. Arrange on a plate with the roast meat.

Roast pork with vegetable beads
Peel 4 carrots, 4 courgettes and 4 potatoes. Scoop balls out of the vegetables with a Solferino scoop. Heat 2 tbsps butter in a pan. Fry the vegetables in the butter, season with salt and pepper. Use to fill the pre-prepared puff pastry cornets (page 21). Arrange the roast meat on a plate with the pastry cornets.

You don't have to serve up the same old Sunday roast to your guests. With the right accompaniments, you can easily conjure up an original meal.

Roast pork

Serves 4:
1 kg/2 lb 3 oz pork
(shoulder or boneless saddle)
4 tbsps oil
salt
freshly ground black pepper
2 onions
2 cloves garlic
2 carrots
1 sprig rosemary (or ½ tsp dried rosemary)
2 cloves
1 bay leaf
250 ml/8 fl. oz dark beer (stout)
(or salted water)
8 figs
10 fresh vine leaves (or from a jar)

Basic recipe

Approx. 3400 kJ/810 kcal per person

Preparation time: approx. 2 hours

1. Pat the meat dry with kitchen paper, brush with 2 tbsps oil, season with salt and pepper. Preheat the oven to 225° C/425°F/Gas mark 7.

2. Peel the onions and the garlic and divide into 8. Wash, peel and coarsely dice the carrots.

3. Heat the remaining oil in a covered roaster or casserole. Brown and seal the meat all over. Wash the rosemary, shake dry and chop finely. Add to the meat with the cloves, bay leaf and vegetables. Cover with the beer and braise in the centre of the oven for about 1½ hours. Baste occasionally with the stock.

4. Meanwhile carefully remove the bloom from the figs by rubbing with kitchen paper. Cut off the stalk and cut through the figs in a cross shape. Approximately 10 minutes before the end of cooking time, add the figs to the casserole and braise. Remove the meat and slice. Arrange on a plate with the figs and vine leaves.

5. Pass the stock through a sieve. Season to taste with salt and pepper and serve separately with the meat.

▪ Serve with potato straws.

If you carve a joint correctly and arrange it nicely on a plate, this in itself is decorative. Decoratively carved vegetables are an ideal accompaniment to meat.

How to carve a joint correctly:

Carving roast meat

1. Let the meat rest for a little while before carving. Place the meat on a board.

2. Hold the meat still with a meat fork. Using a big, sharp knife cut through the meat, cutting across the grain, in thin slices.

3. Layer the slices of meat (like roof tiles) on a large serving dish.

Cutting meat to be stuffed

1. Cut lengthways through the middle of the meat with a very sharp knife. Fold the narrow, cut section away from the main joint.

2. Cut through the remaining thicker piece in the same way and unfold the meat to make a long thin strip.

3. Once the meat has been stuffed (for example, with herbs, vegetables, dried prunes or roast veal) roll up the meat again.

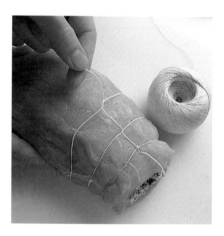

4. Tie up the stuffed roast with kitchen thread to form a "parcel".

Decorative ideas for meat

Chilli flowers
Wash a chilli pod and leave to dry. Using a sharp knife, cut through the pod several times from the tip to the stalk. Remove the seeds from the centre. Place in cold water so that the flowers open out.

Potato mushrooms
Peel a potato and, using a large melon baller, scoop out potato balls. These are the mushroom heads. To make the stalks, cut out one side of the ball using an apple corer. Sauté in butter.

Onion flowers
Remove the skin from a nice, large onion. Cut off a small slice at top and bottom. Slice the outer layer into 8 petal-shaped sections. Don't slice all the way through – the petals should still be connected to the base of the onion. Cut 2 further layers in the same way. Place the onion in iced water, so the flower can open up.

Kohlrabi flower
Peel a kohlrabi, then cut off a slice at top and bottom so it stands flat. Using the tip of a vegetable peeler or an apple corer, work from the top to the bottom, scooping out little circles to form flower petals all around the vegetable.

Tip
Large mushrooms and beetroot can also be shaped into flowers.

Lamb rolls in strudel pastry

Serves 4:
350 g/12 oz fillet of lamb
2 cloves garlic
3 tbsps cold-pressed olive oil
salt
freshly ground black pepper
500 g/1 lb 2 oz leaf spinach
50 g/2 oz ready-made strudel pastry
(or filo pastry)
100 ml/3 fl. oz lamb stock (from cube)
200 g/7 oz double cream
30 g/1 oz pine kernels
For frying:
fat

Approx. 2500 kJ/600 kcal per person

Preparation time: approx. 1 hour

1. Cut the lamb fillet into 4 strips. Peel the garlic cloves and crush using a knife or a garlic press. Mix with the oil. Brush the meat with 1 tbsp of the oil mixture, season with salt and pepper.

2. Wash and clean the spinach. Blanch the leaves in boiling water. Leave to dry on kitchen paper.

3. Using a knife, stretch the slices of meat until flat. Place about ⅓ of the spinach on the strips of meat and roll up.

4. Spread the strudel pastry out on a damp cloth and cut out circles. They must be bigger than the lamb rolls. Brush with 1 tbsp garlic oil, place 1 lamb roll in the centre of each circle, gather up the edges of each pastry circle and press the seams tightly together.

5. Mix the lamb stock and cream together in a pan, bring to the boil and cook at a fast boil until reduced to a thick sauce. Heat the remaining garlic oil, add the spinach to the pan and heat through. Season with salt and pepper. Roast the pine kernels, without fat, in a frying pan.
6. Heat the oil for frying. Carefully fry the rolls in the oil for about 8 minutes until the pastry is golden brown. Remove from pan and drain on kitchen paper.

7. Divide the spinach among the plates. Sprinkle pine kernels on top. Place the rolls in the middle. Serve the sauce separately.

Stuffed fillet of pork

Serves 4:
2 pork fillets (each approx. 250 g)/9 oz
200 g/7 oz kumquats
2 leeks
salt
freshly ground black pepper
1 tbsp oil
2 tbsps clarified butter
kitchen thread

Approx. 1400 kJ/330 kcal per person

Preparation time: approx. 1 hour

1. Preheat the oven to 220° C/425°F/Gas mark 7.

2. Slice the pork fillets, using a sharp knife, so they are ready for stuffing (page 88). Wash the kumquats and pat dry. Slit the leek up the middle, wash thoroughly, cut off the green leaves and blanch these quickly in boiling water.

3. Sprinkle the pork fillets with salt and pepper and brush with oil. Place a nice green leek leaf on each fillet, then divide about half of the kumquats between the fillets. Fold over the fillets and sew up using kitchen thread.

4. Heat the clarified butter in a casserole. Fry the fillets in the butter until crisp and brown. Transfer casserole to oven and bake in centre for about 5 minutes, then turn oven down to 200° C/400°F/Gas mark 6.

Roast the fillets for a further 15 minutes.

5. In the meantime, cut the remaining leek in half lengthways, and cut into 3 cm/1 inch long pieces. Slice the remaining kumquats. About 5 minutes before the end of cooking time, add the leek and kumquats to the meat in the casserole.

6. Cut the fillets into slices, arrange on plates with the leek and kumquats.

Tip
You can use preserved kumquats instead of fresh.

Quick to cook, lovely to look at

The following recipes are all based on 4 steaks. A beef steak (200 g)/7 oz contains about 1050 kJ/252 kcal, a pork steak (150 g)/6 oz about 1100 kJ/264 kcal.

How to prepare the steaks:
Fry the steaks in hot oil for about 5 minutes per side. Remove from pan, season with salt and pepper and then continue according to individual recipes.

Steaks with herb butter

Serves 4:
4 tinned artichoke hearts
100 g/4 oz butter
1 tbsp mixed chopped herbs
1 tsp lime juice
salt
freshly ground white pepper
1 lime

Approx. 870 kJ/210 kcal per person

Preparation time: about 10 minutes

1. Remove the artichoke hearts from the tin and drain.

2. Mix the butter, which should be at room temperature, with the herbs and the lime juice. Season with salt and pepper. Put herb butter in a piping bag with a star-shaped nozzle and pipe onto the artichoke hearts.

3. Wash the lime in hot water, and cut into slices. Place the artichoke heart on top of a slice of lime and serve with the steak.

Steaks with green beans

Serves 4:
300 g/11 oz dwarf beans
salt
vinegar
2 thin rashers bacon
2 tbsps butter
freshly ground black pepper

Approx. 460 kJ/110 kcal per person

Preparation time: approx. 20 minutes

1. Wash the beans and remove any strings. Bring water to the boil in a large saucepan with the salt and a dash of vinegar. Blanch the beans for 5 minutes. Remove and leave to drain.

2. Cut 8 beans into 4, lengthways. Reserve for garnish.

3. Divide the remaining beans into 4 portions. Cut the slices of bacon in half lengthways. Wrap a strip of bacon around each portion of beans.

4. Heat the butter and sauté the beans briefly in it. Season with salt and pepper. Arrange the beans on a plate with the steak and decorate with strips of bean.

Steak with broccoli

Serves 4:
2 large apples
1 tbsp lemon juice
300 g/11 oz broccoli (fresh or frozen)
1 tbsp nibbed almonds
1 tbsp butter

Approx. 320 kJ/76 kcal per person

Preparation time: approx. 15 minutes

1. Peel the apples, remove the core using an apple corer. Cut the apple into slices and drizzle with lemon juice.

2. Defrost the frozen broccoli if used. Clean fresh broccoli. Then divide into small florets.

3. Roast the almonds in a frying pan, without fat.

4. Heat the butter, sauté the broccoli briefly in the butter. Place the broccoli on top of the slices of apple, sprinkle with almonds and arrange on plates with the steaks.

Steak with baby onions

Serves 4:
16 baby onions (chippolini or other small round onions, such as shallots)
2 tbsps butter
1 tbsp sugar
1 bunch flat-leaf parsley
For frying:
fat
4 metal or wooden skewers

Approx. 440 kJ/100 kcal per person

Preparation time: approx. 15 minutes

1. Peel the onion. Heat the butter in a pan, add the sugar and 100 ml/3 fl. oz water and bring to boil.

2. Add the onions to the pan and simmer for 5 minutes.

3. Wash the parsley, pat dry and remove from stalks. Heat the fat for frying, quickly sauté the parsley in it.

4. Remove the onions from the pan, and spear 4 onions on each skewer. Arrange on a plate with the steaks and garnish with parsley.

Veal ragout

Serves 4:
750 g/1 lb 11 oz veal
lemon pepper
salt
2 tbsps flour
30 g/1 oz morel mushrooms
125 ml/4 fl. oz white wine
2 tbsps butter or oil
250 ml/8 fl. oz ready-made veal stock
1 tsp Worcestershire sauce
250 g/9 oz cream

Approx. 2000 kJ/480 kcal per person

Preparation time: approx. 1½ hours

1. Cut the meat into 2 cm/1 inch dice.
Season with salt and pepper and dust
with 1 tbsp flour. Wash the morels and
pour the wine over them.

2. Melt the butter in a large pan. Fry
the meat in the butter in batches and
keep warm. Add the veal stock to the
pan with the meat residues and bring
to the boil until the meat residues have
been incorporated into the sauce.
Strain through a sieve and return to
the pan.

3. Add the morels, wine,
Worcestershire sauce and approx. ⅔ of
the cream to the pan. Place the meat in
the sauce and simmer for about 1
hour.

4. Mix the remaining cream with the
leftover flour and stir into the ragout.
Season to taste.

▪ Serve the ragout on a bed of pasta
verdi.

Top: game stew in a corn ring
Bottom: veal ragout

Variations:
The stew looks pretty in a moulded ring of rice (wild rice mixed with plain boiled rice). Garnish with tomato roses.

Game stew in a corn ring

Serves 6:
For the stew:
750 g/1 lb 11 oz game
salt
freshly ground black pepper
2 tbsps flour
100 g/4 oz streaky bacon
2 tbsps oil
1 large onion
250 ml/8 fl. oz game stock
3 juniper berries
2 bay leaves
1 tsp thyme
1 tsp black peppercorns
500 ml/16 fl. oz red wine
250 g/9 oz chestnuts (tinned)
250 g/9 oz shallots
2 tbsps butter
1 tbsp sugar
For the corn ring:
1.5 l/2½ pints stock
300 g/11 oz corn meal or polenta
1 tbsp oil
sprigs of thyme

Approx. 2850 kJ/676 kcal per person

Preparation time: approx. 2 hours

1. For the stew, cut the meat into 2 cm/1 inch chunks. Season with salt and pepper and dust with flour. Dice the bacon. Heat the oil in a pan, fry the diced bacon until crisp and brown and remove from pan.

2. Peel and finely dice the onions. Fry gently in the hot oil until transparent. Then fry the meat in batches. Add the game stock. Also add the juniper berries, bay leaves, thyme and peppercorns. Simmer for about 10 minutes. Pour the red wine into the pan and braise for a further hour.

3. Peel the shallots. Melt the butter in a saucepan. Gradually add the sugar. Stir until the sugar has dissolved. Drain the chestnuts and seal them in the butter with the shallots.

4. Add the chestnuts, shallots and diced bacon to the stew; braise together for a further 30 minutes.

5. To make the corn ring, bring the stock to the boil in a pan with a thick base and gradually add the corn meal in a trickle, stirring all the time. Leave to swell over a low heat for about 40 minutes. Stir occasionally.

6. Brush a ring mould with oil. Fill the mould with the corn meal, pressing down firmly. There shouldn't be any air pockets. Turn out onto a large serving dish.

7. Adjust seasoning in stew, pour into the middle of the corn ring and serve, garnished with fresh thyme.

Variation:
Serve the stew with mashed potato, garnished with pumpkin leaves stuffed with cranberries.

Baked chicken leg portions

An original approach to serving chicken legs is to arrange legs prepared using different recipes next to each other on a tray or serving dish.

Chicken in a herb crust

Ingredients for 4 portions:
4 fresh chicken legs
1 tsp medium hot mustard
2 tbsps ready-made pesto
1 tbsp chopped parsley

Approx. 860 kJ/200 kcal per leg

Preparation time: approx. 35 minutes

1. Preheat the oven to 220° C/425°F/Gas mark 7.

2. Wash the chicken portions and pat dry. Spread mustard over chicken. Mix the pesto with the parsley. Spread pesto mixture over chicken legs.

3. Line a baking sheet with baking parchment, bake the chicken legs in the centre of the oven for about 25-30 minutes.

Curried chicken legs

Ingredients for 4 portions:
4 fresh chicken legs
2 tbsps oil
1 tsp curry powder
½ tsp turmeric
mace
salt

Approx. 880 kJ/210 kcal per leg

Preparation time: approx. 35 minutes (+ 30 minutes marinating time)

1. Preheat the oven to 220° C/425°F/ Gas mark 7.

2. Wash the chicken portions and pat dry. Mix together the oil, curry, turmeric and a pinch of mace. Season with salt to taste. Brush the chicken portions with about ⅔ of the mixture, cover, and leave to marinate for about 30 minutes.

3. Line a baking sheet with baking parchment, place the chicken portions on the sheet. Bake in the centre of the oven for about 25-30 minutes. Brush with the remaining marinade from time to time.

Honeyed chicken legs

Ingredients for 4 portions:
4 fresh chicken legs
1 tbsp honey
2 tbsps soy sauce
1 tbsp sesame oil
chilli powder

Approx. 850 kJ/200 kcal per leg

Preparation time: approx. 35 minutes (+ 30 minutes marinating time)

1. Preheat the oven to 220° C/425°F/ Gas mark 7.

2. Wash the chicken portions and pat dry. Gently heat the honey. Mix with the soy sauce, sesame oil and a pinch of chilli. Brush the chicken portions with about ⅔ of the mixture, cover and leave to marinate for about 30 minutes.

3. Line a baking sheet with baking parchment, place the chicken portions on the sheet. Bake in the centre of the oven for about 25-30 minutes. Brush with the remaining honey marinade from time to time.

Tip
This looks pretty if you mix romana lettuce with radish sprouts and arrange on a plate with the chicken legs.

Desserts

Desserts are the icing on the cake. None of your guests will be able to resist an enticing fruity, creamy or melt-in-the-mouth dessert, even after a filling main course. Whether you opt for refreshing melon, speedy mousses or the more laborious petit fours, each one still guarantees a feast for the eyes.

Red berry compôte with vanilla foam

Serves 6:
400 g/14 oz cherries (from a jar)
300 g/11 oz mixed berry fruits
(fresh or frozen)
60 g/2 oz caster sugar
1 vanilla pod
½ cinnamon stick
40 g/2 oz cornflour
40 ml/approx. 1 fl. oz raspberry
liqueur
500 ml/16 fl. oz bottled cherry juice
50 g/2 oz icing sugar
1 tbsp cherry brandy
4 leaves gelatine
1 sachet vanilla sauce mix
400 ml/13 fl. oz milk
125 g/5 oz cream
mint leaves

Approx. 1500 kJ/360 kcal per person

Preparation time: approx. 45 minutes
(+ 3 hours chilling time)

1. To make the red berry compôte, put the cherries in a sieve and leave to drain. Reserve the juice.

2. Wash the berries; if necessary cut into smaller pieces. If you are using frozen berries, leave them to defrost.

3. Make up the juice from the cherries to 500 ml/16 fl. oz with water and pour into a large saucepan. Add the sugar, vanilla pod and cinnamon stick and bring everything to the boil. Mix the cornflour with a little water, and add to the boiling cherry juice, stirring all the time. Remove the vanilla pod and the cinnamon stick.

4. Put the fruit into the pan and simmer gently for about 2 minutes. Flavour with the raspberry liqueur and refrigerate for about 1 hour.

5. To make the fruit jellies, heat the bottled cherry juice in a pan. Add the icing sugar and cherry brandy and leave to infuse for about 5 minutes.

6. Soften the gelatine in cold water, drain, then dissolve in the cherry juice. Pour the juice into little moulds or expresso cups which have been rinsed out with cold water. Leave to set for about 3 hours.

7. Make up the vanilla sauce with the milk according to the instructions on the packet. Leave to cool a little. Whip the cream until it stands in soft peaks and fold into the vanilla sauce.

8. Carefully loosen the fruit jellies from the moulds and turn out onto a plate. Arrange the red berry compôte attractively next to the jellies. Decorate with mint leaves. Serve the vanilla foam separately.

Exotic fruit jelly

Serves 6:
2 limes
375 ml/12 fl. oz freshly squeezed
orange juice
125 ml/4 fl. oz white wine
60 g/2 oz icing sugar
3 star anise
zest of 1 orange
6 leaves gelatine
20 ml/1 tbsp orange liqueur
2 kiwi fruit
1 mango
1 star fruit
2 oranges
1 tbsp icing sugar
lemon balm

Approx. 790 kJ/190 kcal per person

Preparation time: approx. 50 minutes
(+ 2 hours chilling time)

1. Squeeze the limes. Remove the zest from 1 lime in thin strips. Put the lime juice in a pan with the orange juice and white wine. Add the icing sugar, star anise, lime and orange zest. Cover and leave to infuse for about 30 minutes.

2. Soften the gelatine in cold water. Slowly heat the fruit juice and leave to infuse for about 5 minutes. Then remove the star anise and dissolve the gelatine in the juice. Stir in the orange liqueur.

3. Peel the kiwi fruit and mango and slice. Wash and slice the star fruit. Peel the orange, slice, and divide the slices into 4. Mix together the fruit and sieve the icing sugar on top.

4. Arrange the fruit decoratively in a deep glass dish. Pour the fruit jelly over the top and leave to set. Decorate with star anise if liked.

Variations:
Pour the jelly into dessert dishes which have been rinsed out with cold water and leave to set. Then turn out onto a plate, divide the fruit salad decoratively between the jellies. Garnish with lemon balm.
Pour the fruit jelly into a large shallow mould. Leave to set. Then cut out dice, diamonds or other shapes. Arrange decoratively with the fruit salad.

Garnish tip
Garnish the exotic fruit salad with edible flowers (e.g. wild violets, daisies or rose petals).

You should serve your guests these fruity desserts on special occasions. The melon is especially good on hot days.

Pineapple with cream filling

Serves 4:
2 ripe baby pineapples (each approx. 500 g)/1 lb 2 oz
100 g/4 oz caster sugar
250 ml/8 fl. oz wine
6 leaves gelatine
375 g/13 oz cream
50 g/2 oz plain chocolate

Approx. 2200 kJ/520 kcal per person

Preparation time: approx. 45 minutes

1. Cut the pineapple and stalk in half lengthways. Using a pointed knife remove the flesh and cut into small pieces. Reserve a few pieces for decoration.

2. Put the remaining fruit with the sugar and half of the wine in a pan. Bring to the boil and simmer for about 8 minutes. Leave to cool a little, then purée.

3. Soften the gelatine in cold water according to the instructions on the packet. Add the remaining wine to the fruit purée, heat gently and dissolve the gelatine in it. Refrigerate until the mixture begins to set.

4. Whip the cream until stiff. Gradually fold the fruit purée into the cream. Put the pineapple cream in a piping bag with a large round nozzle and pipe into the pineapple halves.

5. Melt the chocolate in a bowl over hot water, and use to brush onto the edges of the reserved pineapple pieces. Decorate the filled pineapples with the chocolate coated chunks and serve immediately.

Filled melons

Serves 6:
1 large watermelon
1 honeydew melon
1 ogen melon
1 cantaloupe melon
20 ml/1 tbsp brandy
1 tbsp icing sugar

Approx. 500 kJ/120 kcal per person

1. Wash the watermelon and cut off a lid; slice across the bottom of the melon so it stands flat. Decorate the edge of the melon with a zig-zag pattern. Using a potato peeler or a metal skewer, carve a pattern in the melon rind. Using a large melon baller, scoop out the flesh. Discard the seeds.

2. Cut the other melons in half and scoop out the flesh with a melon baller.

3. Drizzle brandy over the melon balls and dust with icing sugar.

4. Fill the hollowed-out watermelon with the fruit salad and serve.

Variation:
The melon can also be filled with papaya, mango, lychees, kiwi fruit and cherries.

Tip
How to tell if a melon is ripe:
Ogen, honeydew and cantaloupe melons are ripe when they are heavily perfumed and if the stalk end "gives" if you press down lightly on it. A watermelon is ripe if you rap on it and it doesn't sound hollow.

The cutting technique is important here. It just takes a few cuts for fruit to be transformed into great decorations.

Pineapple slices and chunks

1. Cut away the upper part of the pineapple. Cut a slice off the bottom so the pineapple will stand upright. Place the pineapple on a board and cut away the peel in slices from top to bottom. Using a pointed knife, remove the "eyes".

2. The pineapple eyes are arranged in spirals; they can easily be removed if you cut spiral grooves in the pineapple. In this way the pineapple slices will also have an attractively scalloped edge.

3. Slice the pineapple. Using a round cutter, cut out the hard stalk. Then cut into chunks if liked.

4. A special pineapple knife makes the job very easy. You position it on top of the pineapple like a corkscrew and it cuts away the stalk and skin. Unfortunately this piece of kitchen equipment is not widely available.

Filling pineapples
To fill a pineapple, cut the fruit in half lengthways, remove the stalk and scoop out the flesh.

Baby pineapple spirals

1. Even up the base of the pineapple.

2. Using a serrated knife, and starting from the bottom, thickly cut away the pineapple skin in a spiral, until the pineapple has no skin left on it.

Mango slices

1. Peel away the mango skin from top to bottom.

2. Divide the mango in half lengthways. Remove the stone.

3. Place the mango flat, cut side down, and slice.

Mango flowers

1. Cut away the mango flesh on either side, cutting close to the stone.

2. Place the mango halves peel side down on a board. Cut the flesh in a chess-board pattern, but don't cut right through to the skin.

3. Take the mango halves in both hands and press gently but firmly on the mango skin from underneath so that the middle is pushed in and the squares of flesh on top are pushed upwards and outwards to form a flower.

Apple notches

1. Take a red apple with a pretty skin, wash and divide into quarters. Remove the core so that the surface is flat.

2. Now cut a small notch in the middle of the peel.

3. Make another cut next to the first one so that there is a narrow border between the 2. Repeat the same process twice more. Take care that the cut sections don't fall apart.

4. Sprinkle with lemon juice and reassemble again to one side.

Filleting oranges

1. Cut away the rind of an orange with a sharp knife in a spiral.

2. Divide the orange into sections.

3. Cut away the membrane from the orange slices.

Decorations for melon rind

• Cut off a lid. Decorate the lid and melon rind using a pointed knife or a small metal skewer.

• Cut off a lid. Using a round cutter, mark a scallop pattern around the edge of the melon and then cut out.

• Cut the melon in half and, using a sharp pointed knife, decorate each of the halves with a sawtooth pattern.

• Using a linoleum knife or wood carving knife, carve patterns, flowers and letters in the melon rind.

Mousse – naughty, but nice

Mousse, a delicate sweet cream, will be accepted enthusiastically after even the most substantial meal.

Chocolate mousse

Serves 4:
2 eggs
1 tbsp icing sugar
1 tbsp cognac or rum if liked
200 g/7 oz plain chocolate
20 g/1 oz butter
250 g/9 oz cream

Basic recipe

Approx. 2400 kJ/570 kcal per person

Preparation time: approx. 20 minutes (+ at least 6 hours chilling time)

1. In a bowl over hot water, whisk the eggs, icing sugar and brandy or rum together until foamy.

2. Coarsely chop the chocolate, melt in a bowl over hot water with the butter and stir into the eggs. Leave to cool.

3. Whip the cream until stiff. Carefully fold into the egg mixture. Cover and leave to chill, overnight if possible.

White mousse

Serves 4:
2 leaves gelatine
2 eggs
1 tbsp icing sugar
1 tbsp white rum if liked
200 g/7 oz white chocolate
250 g/9 oz cream

Approx. 2200 kJ/520 kcal per person
Preparation time: approx. 20 minutes (+ at least 6 hours chilling time)

1. Soften the gelatine in cold water. In a bowl over hot water, whisk the eggs, icing sugar and rum until foamy.

2. Melt the chocolate in a bowl over hot water. Drain the gelatine. Add both to the egg mixture. Leave to cool.

3. Whip the cream until stiff and carefully fold into the egg mixture. Cover and refrigerate overnight.

Variation:
Peppermint mousse
Instead of the rum use a mint-flavoured liqueur and decorate with mint leaves.

Blackcurrant mousse

Serves 4:
300 g/11 oz blackcurrants
60 g/2 oz icing sugar
2 leaves gelatine
1 tbsp blackcurrant liqueur (crème de cassis)
1 tbsp cherry brandy, if liked
2 eggs
200 g/7 oz cream

Approx. 1300 kJ/310 kcal per person

Preparation time: approx. 30 minutes (+ at least 6 hours chilling time)

1. Wash the blackcurrants, clean and bring to the boil with the icing sugar for about 3 minutes. Soften the gelatine.

2. Pass the fruit through a sieve and stir the drained gelatine into the warm fruit purée. Stir in the blackcurrant liqueur and cherry brandy. Leave to cool a little.

3. Meanwhile, in a bowl over hot water, whisk the eggs until white and fluffy. Fold in the fruit purée. Whip the cream until stiff and fold in.

4. Refrigerate overnight, if possible.

Variations:
The mousse can also be made with strawberries or raspberries.

Tip
White and dark chocolate mousse arranged on a glass plate achieve a pretty effect. Decorate with curls of white and dark chocolate, or take scoops of different types of mousse and arrange them on a dessert plate. Decorate with whipped cream and fruit. Another alternative is to arrange on a plate with softly whipped cream and white and dark chocolate leaves.

Goes with mousse:
Fruit purée (coulis)
Put 300 g/11 oz frozen mixed fruits in a pan with 60 g/2 oz icing sugar, bring to boil and simmer for about 3 minutes. Pass through a sieve and refrigerate. To serve, pour a lake of fruit purée onto a serving dish or plate, then place scoops of mousse on top of the coulis.

Frosted blackcurrants
Dip washed blackcurrants in lemon juice, then dredge in sugar.

Top: blackcurrant mousse
Bottom: chocolate mousse and white mousse

Chocolate with everything!

Plain, milk and white chocolate are suitable for chocolate coatings.

To melt the chocolate, take the required type and break into small pieces. Melt in a bowl over hot water.

• To make curls (caraque)

1. Allow the melted chocolate to cool a little. Pour onto a large flat plate or marble board brushed with oil.

2. Allow the coating of chocolate to set a little.

3. Using a small spatula, palette knife or broad-bladed knife, push the blade along the chocolate to form curls.

• Cutting out shapes

1. Line a flat dish or mould with baking parchment. Pour in the melted chocolate to a depth of about ½ cm / ¼ inch. Allow the coating of chocolate to set.

2. Carefully remove from mould. Cut out shapes with decorative cutters or using a knife and templates.

• Chocolate leaves

1. Take some rose leaves or other leaves, wash and dry thoroughly on kitchen paper.

2. Hold the leaves by the stem and dip one side in melted chocolate. Place the leaves with the chocolate side uppermost on baking parchment. Leave to set.

3. Carefully pull the green leaves away from the chocolate, working from the stem up. Make the chocolate leaves out of dark and white chocolate.

• Fruits in chocolate

Dip half of a Cape gooseberry (physalis) in melted chocolate; cherries with their stalks should be coated completely or halfway up; and coat strawberries completely. Cut star fruit into slices and brush the edges with a thin layer of melted chocolate.

• Chocolate decorations

1. Make little piping bags out of greaseproof paper. Cut out a greaseproof paper triangle. Roll up to form a cornet. Fold over the edges, so that the cornet holds together.

2. Fill the cornet with melted chocolate. Cut off the tip of the cornet. Pipe filigree patterns and decorations onto baking parchment or the dish to be decorated.

3. Leave to cool, and carefully remove from paper as necessary.

Tip
Melt a little butter or coconut oil with the chocolate, then it will be easier to work with. You can also fill a small plastic bag with the melted chocolate. Cut a tiny hole, or cut off the corner, with a pair of scissors.

• Chocolate cream (ganache)

1. Heat 100 g/4 oz cream in a pan. Break 200 g/7 oz plain chocolate into pieces and add to the cream. Dissolve, stirring constantly. Leave to cool thoroughly in the refrigerator.

2. Beat the chocolate cream using a whisk or hand mixer. Fill a piping bag with the mixture and, using different decorative nozzles, pipe onto desserts, cakes and other dishes.

• Chocolate strands
The chocolate shouldn't be too cold for this.
Hold a bar of chocolate over a plate or baking parchment. Using a vegetable peeler or a knife, scrape off long strands lengthways.

• Grated chocolate
Chill the chocolate in the refrigerator, then grate in the same way as for vegetables, cheese etc.

A dessert doesn't have to take ages to make. These dishes, made with packet mixes, are quick and easy, and still look good.

Black and white pudding

Serves 6:
1 sachet vanilla blancmange mix
1 sachet chocolate blancmange mix
1 l/1¾ pints milk
4 tbsps caster sugar
200 g/7 oz cream
chocolate leaves (commercially made)

Approx. 1200 kJ/290 kcal per person

Preparation time: approx. 15 minutes
(+ 4 hours chilling time)

1. Prepare both mixes with the milk and sugar according to the instructions on the packet.

2. Layer the dark and light blancmange, whilst still warm, in a shallow mould or dish. Chill.

3. Turn out of mould and cut into dice.

4. Whip the cream until stiff. Arrange the dice on a plate with the cream. Garnish with a few chocolate leaves.

Gugelhupf

Serves 6:
2 sachets vanilla blancmange mix
750 ml/1¼ pints milk
250 g/9 oz cream
160 g/6 oz caster sugar

Approx. 1600 kJ/380 kcal per person

Preparation time: approx. 20 minutes
(+ 4 hours chilling time)

1. Prepare the mix with the milk, cream and 60 g/2 oz sugar, according to the instructions on the packet.

2. Rinse a gugelhupf mould of about 1 l/1¾ pint capacity with cold water. Fill the mould with the blancmange and leave to chill thoroughly in the refrigerator.

3. Turn the pudding out onto a glass plate.

4. Melt the remaining sugar in a heavy-based pan with 1 tbsp water, until the sugar turns golden brown. Don't let it boil any more, or the caramel will burn. Using a spoon, spin sugar threads out of the syrup, on top of the blancmange.

Variation:
Melt 50 g/2 oz plain chocolate in a bowl over hot water. Fill a small freezer bag with the melted chocolate. Cut a tiny hole and pipe the chocolate in a spiral pattern over the blancmange.

Vanilla blancmange with strawberries

Serves 4:
1 sachet vanilla blancmange mix
200 ml/7 fl. oz milk
100 g/4 oz crème fraiche
2 tbsps sugar
250 g/9 oz strawberries
1 tbsp lemon juice
1 tbsp icing sugar

Approx. 950 kJ/230 kcal per person

Preparation time: approx. 20 minutes
(+ 4 hours chilling time)

1. Prepare the blancmange with the milk, crème fraiche and sugar according to the instructions on the packet.

2. Rinse 4 individual savarin moulds or other dessert moulds with cold water. Fill the moulds with blancmange and refrigerate for at least 4 hours.

3. Wash the strawberries, hull and leave to dry completely. Reserve a few strawberry leaves. Chop the fruit into small dice and marinate in the lemon juice and icing sugar.

4. Turn the blancmange out onto a plate. Arrange with the strawberries and garnish with strawberry leaves.

Petit fours

These small, lovingly decorated cakes are traditionally served with coffee in France as the perfect end to a meal.

Makes about 20 petit fours:
For the cake:
6 eggs
salt
300 g/11 oz caster sugar
80 g/3 oz flour
100 g/4 oz ground almonds
For the filling:
300 g/11 oz marzipan
150 g/6 oz icing sugar
2 tsps almond liqueur if liked
400 g/14 oz apricot jam
baking parchment
cling film
For decoration
2 egg whites
500 g/1 lb 2 oz icing sugar
1 tsp lemon juice
food colouring
candied flowers
glacé cherries
pistachio nuts
chocolate

Approx. 1700 kJ/400 kcal per petit four

Preparation time: approx. 2 hours (+ 24 hours chilling time)

1. Preheat the oven to 200° C/400°F/ Gas mark 6. Line a baking sheet with baking parchment.

2. To make the fatless sponge mixture, separate the eggs. Whisk the egg whites with a pinch of salt until stiff. Gradually stir in 50 g/2 oz sugar. Whisk the remaining sugar, except for 2 tsps, with the egg yolks until foamy.

3. Pile the egg whites on top of the egg yolk mixture, sieve the flour on top, and carefully fold in everything using a wooden spoon. Finally fold in the almonds. Spread the mixture evenly over the baking sheet and bake in the centre of the oven for about 15 minutes.

4. Take a cloth or a sheet of baking parchment the same size as the baking sheet and sprinkle the remaining sugar on top. Turn the sponge out onto the sugared cloth or paper and leave to cool. Then cut into 3 even strips.

5. To make the filling, knead the marzipan together with the icing sugar and almond liqueur. Roll out between cling film. Cut into 2 strips the same size as the sponge strips.

6. Warm the apricot jam in a pan, pass through a sieve and spread 1 of the sponge strips with ⅓ of the jam. Place the second layer of sponge on top, spread the next ⅓ of jam on top and cover with a strip of marzipan. Place the third layer of sponge on top, cover with the remaining jam and marzipan. Then wrap in foil or baking parchment, weigh down with a board and refrigerate for at least 24 hours. The separate layers must merge together properly.

7. Next day remove the board and paper. Cut the sponge into small squares, circles, rectangles and diamonds.

8. To make the decoration, whisk the egg whites until stiff, stir in the icing sugar and lemon juice. The mixture should be thick. Colour with food colouring as liked.

9. Place a wire rack on top of a sheet of baking parchment or foil. Using a spoon, coat the petit fours evenly with the different-coloured icings. Place on the wire rack and leave to dry.

10. Make some small paper piping bags. Cut a tiny hole in the tip of each. Fill the piping bags with different coloured icing and pipe patterns onto the petit fours. Then decorate with candied flowers, cherries, pistachio nuts and chocolate as liked.

Tip
Instead of royal icing you could use ready-made fondant icing, which you can buy from most supermarkets. You should only use very fresh egg whites for royal icing.

How to make petit fours step by step is on pages 114-115.

Petit fours made easy

1. Using a large knife, cut the cooked, cooled sponge base into 3 even-sized strips.

2. Brush each of the 3 strips of sponge with jam and layer alternately with the marzipan. Then everything must be left for 24 hours to combine.

3. Make the royal icing, divide into 3 portions, and colour each portion with a different-coloured food colouring.

4. Place the cut-out sponge shapes on a wire rack and coat with icing. Leave the icing to dry.

5. Using piping bags made out of baking parchment, decorate the petit fours with coloured or chocolate icing. You can pipe classic decorations or use your imagination.

6. Specialist shops offer a wide range of decorations – candied violets, rose leaves, cherries, sugar decorations, angelica and coloured marzipan.

7. If you are fairly skilled you can make marzipan roses yourself. Colour marzipan with food colouring and then use to make petals and leaves.

8. It is also very easy to candy flowers yourself. Suitable flowers are roses, hydrangeas and violets. The following recipe will show you how.

Candied roses

A rose which has just opened, with stems and leaves.
1 egg white or 2 tbsps lemon juice
150 g/6 oz caster sugar
icing sugar

1. Leave the rose to dry thoroughly.

2. Beat the egg white with 1 tbsp water or put the lemon juice in a small bowl.

3. Dip the flowers and leaves in the egg white or lemon juice. Carefully swish about in the egg white. Remove and leave to drain.

4. Sprinkle sugar on both sides of the leaves. Dust the inside of the flower, then the outside, with caster sugar. Hang up to dry in a warm room. Before using dust with a little icing sugar.

Christa Schmedes' love of cooking took her into the hotel trade; she served her cookery apprenticeship in Baden, Germany, an area with a high culinary reputation. Christa now lives in Munich, and for the past ten years she has been a freelance contributor to the test kitchens of major newspapers and cookbook publishers. She specialises in creating tasty recipes and exquisite menus that can be prepared quickly using simple ingredients.

Pete A. Eising and Susanne Eising specialise exclusively in food photography. Their client base includes advertising agencies and industrial companies, magazines and cookbook publishers. Their photographic studio has close links with an international photo agency which also concentrates on food photography. Martina Görlach is responsible for equipment and props at the studio, and also assists with the photographic styling.

Translated from the German by Karen Green
in association with First Edition Translations Limited, Cambridge, UK
Editor: Birgit Rademacker
Photography: Foodfotografie Eising
Styling: Hans Gerlach, Tim Landsberg